FOUNDATIONS OF CHRISTIAN EDUCATION

ADDRESSES TO CHRISTIAN TEACHERS

BY
LOUIS BERKHOF
AND
CORNELIUS VAN TIL

EDITED BY
DENNIS E. JOHNSON

Presbyterian and Reformed Publishing Company
Phillipsburg, New Jersey

These addresses were originally part of a larger volume,
Fundamentals in Christian Education: Theory and Practice,
edited by Cornelius Jaarsma, published in 1953 by William B. Eerdmans.

This collection reprinted in 1990 by Presbyterian and Reformed Publishing Company.

Manufactured in the United States of America.

Set in Palatino by Olive Tree Graphics.

Library of Congress Cataloging-in-Publication Data

Berkhof, Louis, 1873–1957.
Foundations of Christian education: addresses to Christian teachers/ by Louis Berkhof and Cornelius Van Til; edited by Dennis E. Johnson.
p. cm.
"These addresses were originally part of a larger volume, *Fundamentals in Christian Education: Theory and Practice,* edited by Cornelius Jaarsma, published in 1953 by William B. Eerdmans"—T. P. verso.
ISBN 0-87552-114-2
1. Education (Christian theology) 2. Christian education—Philosophy. 3. Reformed Church—Doctrines. 4. Reformed Church—Education. I. Van Til, Cornelius, 1895–1987. II. Johnson, Dennis E. (Dennis Edward) III. Title.
BT738.17.B47 1989
268′.85—dc20 89–39157
CIP

CONTENTS

EDITOR'S PREFACE

The essays contained in this book were originally addresses delivered to national conventions of the National Union of Christian Schools (now Christian Schools International). They first appeared in print as part of a much larger collection entitled *Fundamentals in Christian Education: Theory and Practice* and edited by Cornelius Jaarsma, then professor of education at Calvin College (Grand Rapids: William B. Eerdmans, 1953).

When these addresses were delivered in the 1920s and 1930s, non-parochial (i.e., non-Roman Catholic or non-Lutheran) Christian day schools were a rare phenomenon on the American scene, and it would be no understatement to observe that most evangelical Christians, including many in churches confessing Reformed theology, saw little need to challenge the adequacy of state-controlled public education. It is not surprising, then, that we hear from these authors a tone that is both polemical and encouraging: *polemical*, because the teachers and supporters involved in Christian schools needed then (as we need now) to be reminded constantly that these schools—such costly alternatives in time, money, and energy in comparison to the tax-supported public school down the street—are in fact part of the great spiritual warfare between Christ and Satan, the City of God and the City of Man; and *encouraging*, because those committed to Christian schools needed then (as we need now, but perhaps even more so in those early days) the reassurance that, despite the apparent weakness of their cause in terms of numbers, the Lord of hosts would honor his people's humble efforts, in dependence on his grace, to nurture their children in the Lord's instruction—through all the breadth of the created order, through every moment of human history, experience, and thought.

The Christian school movement in the United States and Canada has "grown up" significantly in the half-century since these words were first spoken. The polemical points so insightfully made by Van Til and Berkhof at that time have become self-evident to a wider circle of Bible-believing Christians as the humanistic world view underlying governmentally sponsored education has become more and more overt. One might even dare to hope that more Christians are recognizing that there is in fact no neutral ground, in education or anywhere else; that nothing can be taught apart from *some* religious orientation, whether it be Christianity, Hinduism, secular humanism, Marxism, or some other.

To be sure, some parents place their children in Christian schools in the hope of avoiding the world's obvious temptations: drugs, premarital sex and the resulting spread of teen pregnancy and life-threatening disease, violence and other crime. But Van Til and Berkhof point us to a deeper rationale for Christian schools, a rationale that plunges to the root of the issue. For the superficial fruit that so alarms the observer of the public high school must be traced to its root in a world view that takes man as the measure of all things. The purpose for the Christian school is not to facilitate flight from surface symptoms but to counteract the source of the infection that attacks the educational system, as it does our society generally, from within.

These essays, then, deal with the "why" of Christian education. Questions of "how"—the "practical" questions, as we so often think of them—are touched on only in passing. Methodological questions are important, and essays by others in Professor Jaarsma's original collection addressed such issues. But it is also essential, particularly as Christian education benefits from increasing sophistication and technological support, to keep clearly focused on the *purpose* of Christian day school education. Only as we have clarity regarding what our work in Christian education is to *be* and to *accomplish* can we select the methods appropriate to those ends. The questions addressed by Van Til and Berkhof are, then, the most practical ones of all; without clear answers here, we can go nowhere.

There are two reasons for the selection of these essays out of the larger collection, *Fundamentals in Christian Education*, for republication at this time. In the first place the suggestion came from Dr. Van Til himself during the final year of his life. It was, in fact, while the essays were in the process of editing for republication that Dr. Van Til was ushered into the glorious presence of his Lord Jesus Christ on April 17, 1987. Although most well known as professor of apologetics at Westminster Theological Seminary and for his pioneering work in developing a Reformed apologetic that challenges non-Christian thought at its presuppositional foundation, Van Til maintained a lifelong concern for the lower levels of

Christian education. In 1942 he was one of the founders of Philadelphia-Montgomery Christian Academy, which now has over 700 students on campuses in three communities near Philadelphia. The dates of the addresses that follow (1930-33) demonstrate Van Til's commitment to Christian education: in those first years of his teaching at Westminster he traveled annually to the Midwest (Michigan, Illinois, Iowa) to bring encouragement and challenge to Christian school teachers. Moreover, even in his last hospitalization Dr. Van Til asked a Christian friend to check on the status of the essays' preparation for republication. In a note to the editor this friend later observed, "I suppose the republication of those articles could be considered [Van Til's] last request."

The second reason for the republication of these essays is the need for those in the Christian school (and Christian home school) movement to hear afresh the words of encouragement and challenge from these prophetic voices of the recent past. The all-too-visible decay in governmentally controlled education and the corresponding expansion of private education, including Christian and home schools, may tempt us to compare systems primarily in terms of measurable externals: enrollment figures, standardized test scores, college admissions; student patriotism, moral responsibility, and community leadership. But the real difference between Christian schools and all other educational systems, public or private, must be traced back to its source in two antithetical world views: on the one hand, the world view that takes the living God, Creator, Revealer, and Redeemer, as its starting point, listening dependently to his revelation in Scripture, creation, and providence; and, on the other hand, the world view that, explicitly or implicitly, denies that the God of the Bible is the source of all reality and the measure of all truth. From these fundamental starting points all the surface characteristics that mark off Christian education from humanistic education flow (with varying degrees of consistency). Thus it is as important now, when Christian schools in North America appear to enjoy a bloom of success, as it was in the earlier decades of struggling survival to hear the basic issues exposed with clarity by Van Til and Berkhof.

Van Til and Berkhof were particularly qualified to clarify these foundational issues in Christian education. Van Til has been introduced briefly above. In his essays the reader will discern his profound grasp of the deep philosophical issues entailed in the day-to-day life of the Christian school. Louis Berkhof is best known for his landmark distillations of Christian doctrine: *Manual of Christian Doctrine* (1933), *Summary of Christian Doctrine* (1938), and *Systematic Theology* (1939). He taught systematic theology and was president of Calvin Theological Seminary, and then he was president emeritus until his death in 1957. The reader will appreciate the clarity with which Berkhof relates the task of Christian education to the great truths of the Christian faith.

After working with these seven addresses, as they now stand as a unit apart from the other essays in *Fundamentals in Christian Education*, it has seemed to me that a rearrangement of them may help readers to enter into the issues Van Til and Berkhof are addressing. Jaarsma placed Van Til's "Antitheses in Education" in the conclusion of his collection, and it well sums up the issues with which we are concerned. But to my mind this essay, together with Berkhof's "Being Reformed in our Attitude to the Christian School," provides an invaluable *introduction* to this new collection, laying out clearly the rationale—no, the imperative—for Christian education. The other five essays all relate Christian education to one or another of the cardinal doctrines of the Christian faith, and they are ordered "systematically": creation, covenant, faith, authority (Berkhof's essay speaks of the implementation of the teacher's role as discipler and discipliner of students), and finally eschatology (Van Til's "The Full-Orbed Life" dramatically critiques the futility of humanism's attempts to formulate an ultimate educational goal/outcome and affirms the climax of sanctification and joy that is the Christian hope).

In the process of editing these essays for republication I have had the privilege of working from Dr. Van Til's own copy of *Fundamentals in Christian Education*, now in the collection of the Montgomery Library, Westminster Theological Seminary (Pennsylvania). A number of revisions or insertions in Van Til's essays therefore reflect his own handwritten marginal notes at points in which he would perhaps have modified or amplified his wording. Beyond these changes the editorial work on the text has been minimal, consisting in the reworking of certain difficult constructions and the addition of explanatory notes. The goal is not an academically precise "critical edition," but a book in which readers—Christian teachers, Christian parents, friends (and, yes, foes) of Christian education—can hear again the Lord's call to arms and faithfulness, delivered through these faithful servants of his.

Dennis E. Johnson
Escondido, California

PART ONE:
THE NECESSITY AND DISTINCTIVENESS OF CHRISTIAN EDUCATION IN REFORMED PERSPECTIVE

1

ANTITHESES IN EDUCATION

CORNELIUS VAN TIL

The principles by which believers live are squarely opposed to the principles by which unbelievers live. This is true in the field of education as well as in the church. Accordingly we speak of antitheses in education. These antitheses cover the whole educational field. They cover first the field of educational philosophy. This is of basic significance, but is often overlooked. In the second place these antitheses appear in the field of what is to be taught, i.e., the curriculum. Finally these antitheses appear when we consider the child or the young person to be instructed. Under these three aspects we shall try to bring out the antitheses in educational philosophy.

Non-Christians believe that the universe has created God. They have a finite god. Christians believe that God has created the universe. They have a finite universe. Non-Christians therefore are not concerned with bringing the child face to face with God. They want to bring the child face to face with the universe. Non-Christian education is *Godless* education. What is of most importance to us in education, that which is absolutely indispensable to us, is left out entirely.

Godless education ignores or denies that man was created responsible to God. This implies that sin is not a transgression of God's law. Hence Christ did not need to die in our stead. Godless or nontheistic education is therefore also non- or anti-Christian education. Godless, non-Christian education naturally becomes humanistic, i.e., man-centered. If man does not need to live for God, he may live for himself. If then we want a God-centered and truly Christian education, we will have to break away completely from the educational philosophy that surrounds us.

Non-Christians believe that man is surrounded by an absolutely unknowable universe. Man is grasping in the dark, except for the little light that his own mind is radiating as a headlight in the mist. Christians believe that originally man lived in the light of the revelation of God and that in Christ as the fact-revelation and in Scripture as the Word-revelation, man is in principle restored to that true light of God.

Accordingly non-Christian education dashes first this way and then that under the delusion that it has pierced the darkness, or it stops altogether in utter despair. Often non-Christian educators do away with the idea of a definite aim or purpose in education altogether. They talk of "functional adjustment" to one's environment. But if man does not know the road and drives in the mist, why should he "step on the gas"? As Christians we *know* the *purpose* of education. We also *know* what should be the *content* of education. Finally we *know* that a definitely Christian *method* is to be used in the instruction of a definitely Christian content.

Non-Christians believe that insofar as man knows anything, he knows apart from God. Man's mind is not an electric bulb that needs a current if it is to show any light, but it is rather an oil lamp that carries its own supplies. Christians believe that everything is dark unless the current of God's revelation be turned on. We cannot even see any "facts" without this light. Non-Christian teachers will accordingly sometimes think they really have and know the "facts" and can teach the child all about them, and then again when they see that the "facts" are really in the dark they will give up in utter despair. Christian teachers know that not a single "fact" can really be known and therefore really be taught unless placed under the light of the revelation of God. Even the laws of arithmetic cannot be known otherwise.

We need to become more conscious of these basic distinctions. Unless we are conscious of them, we shall never have genuinely Christian schools. To be conscious of these distinctions does *not* mean that we must spend much more time on the direct teaching of religion than on teaching other matters. If we teach religion *indirectly*, everywhere and always, we may need less time to teach religion *directly*. To be conscious of these distinctions *does* mean that the plan of curriculum is to be God-centered. Man exists for God. But in the created universe other things exist for man. Hence in this sense the curriculum must be man-centered. Only thus can it become God-centered.

Non-Christians believe that the personality of the child can develop best if it is not placed face to face with God. Christians believe that the child's personality cannot develop at all unless it is placed face to face with God. Non-Christian education puts the child in a vacuum. In this vacuum the child is expected to grow. The result is that the child dies. Christian education alone really nurtures personality because it alone gives the child air and food.

Non-Christians believe that authority hurts the growth of the child. Christians believe that without authority a child cannot live at all.

Non-Christians do speak of the authority of the "expert," but that is not really authority. Christians want authority that is based upon the idea of God as man's Creator and of Christ as man's Redeemer.

Thus we see that the antithesis touches every phase of education. To try to enforce the idea of the antithesis at one point and to ignore it at others is to waste your energy and your money. We cannot afford this.

I. The Antithesis in Educational Philosophy

The whole Christian church is based upon the antithesis idea. But, if anything, it is still more pointedly true of Christian instruction in particular than of Christianity in general that it is based upon the idea of the antithesis. Oh, yes, I know there are voices heard on every side that we must not always emphasize the negative and the destructive but that we must emphasize rather the positive and the constructive. We are told that such is far wiser in the end. Now we all wish to be positive and constructive. But in this world of sin no Christian individual and no Christian organization can be positive and constructive till *after* they have been negative and destructive. To deny or to ignore this fact is to deny or to ignore the fact of sin. For anyone who recognizes the fact of sin in its unadulterated biblical connotation of insult to God on the part of man under the leadership of the devil, antithesis is in the nature of the case basic to synthesis. He who seeks to bring good tidings and to publish peace, he who calls upon Judah to perform her feasts and pay her vows, is a false prophet unless he offers as a reason for his optimism the assurance that the "wicked one will no more pass through because he is utterly cut off." [1]

The Non-Christian Idea of God

In seeking to bring out something of the antitheses in education we wish first of all to stress the fact that there is really only one antithesis. We may speak of a plurality of antitheses only if we keep in mind that all the differences in educational theory are reducible to a single issue, the question of a personal God.

Every educational program seeks to bring the growing personality that is to be educated into the best possible relation to its environment. But such a term as environment is in itself perfectly colorless. And so if we should say that education is "adjustment of the growing personality to its environment," such a definition would be quite without significance unless one would specify what one means by the environment to which the growing personality is to be adjusted. And when it comes to the question of the meaning of the term "environment," it will be seen at once that the Christian theistic and the nontheistic theories of reality stand diametrically opposed to one another. The former affirms that the environment to which human personality is to be adjusted is ultimately personal, while the latter denies it.

It is true that there are plenty of nontheistic theories of reality which speak of superhuman personality or personalities. But this does not make their views *ultimately personalistic.* No theory of reality can properly be called "personalistic" unless it thinks of God as an absolute personality. It is quite possible and quite common to speak of a personal God and yet not to think of him as absolute. Such a monotheism is not theism in the proper sense of the term any more than an outspoken polytheism is. It is clear that, if the god or gods to whom the child is to be adjusted must themselves be adjusted to a fate or a universe or a reality that is beyond or independent of them, in that case we may just as well look beyond such intermediaries and say that the child must be adjusted to this fate or universe or reality or whatever else we may choose to call that which we think of as most ultimate.

Now it seems to me to be incontrovertible that the educational philosophy of today presupposes an ultimately impersonal and thus antitheistic environment to which the child is to be adjusted. If one searches the pages of modern speculative thought, one may find here and there statements about belief in absolute truth and in absolute verities; and these may then be identified with the term "God" so that men may even speak of God as absolute. But when men speak thus they speak metaphorically. The "God" of modern philosophy is at most an impersonation of certain ideals that men have set for themselves and of which they are ultimately themselves the judges. Accordingly a metaphorical God is for all practical purposes a finite God.

It is to this universe, this reality, then, that the child must be adjusted, according to current educational philosophy; and it is this adjustment that constitutes his education. It follows that we have not grasped the depth of the educational antitheses until we have traced them back to this absolutely determinative antithesis between an ultimately personal and an ultimately impersonal surrounding. And no more basic difference is thinkable. The whole of the educational program built upon an impersonal background must be diametrically opposed to an educational program built upon a personal foundation. We shall seek to bring out something of this below. Suffice it for the moment to call attention to the fact that, for better or worse, every Christian educator should come to grips with this point. And anyone who comes to grips with it at all will sense the impossibility of thinking of Christian education as being ninety or sixty or thirty or ten percent like other education, the only difference being that Christian education adds certain elements or emphasizes certain elements that secular education neglects. When viewed from this absolute standpoint Christian education is not even a fraction of one percent like public education. The different conceptions of God that underlie the two educational theories cover every point on the whole front and cover them before and behind, without and within.

At this point I may interject that when I thus emphasize the absolute antithesis, I am not denying or even for a moment forgetting the doctrine of common grace. That doctrine does not militate against the doctrine of the absolute antithesis, but here as elsewhere confirms it. Common grace does not overlook ultimate differences. Nor does it, when correctly understood, in any way tone down those ultimate differences. On the contrary, common grace helps to point out that things which look alike are not ultimately alike. Common grace points specifically to the fact that similarities between the people of God and the people of this world are but proximate similarities and that these proximate similarities play before the background of ultimate differences. If people do not believe in common grace or do not know what it means, they are likely to raise proximate similarities to ultimate similarities or to raise proximate differences to ultimate differences with the result that the absolute differences are toned down. It is this which has often taken place in non-Reformed churches. There it has been thought that religion is a condiment that may be added to the otherwise neutral territories of life. Because they did not understand the doctrine of common grace these churches took it for granted that no ultimate difference could be hidden behind the statement of a Christian that two times two are four and a statement of a non-Christian that two times two are four.

Now the fact that two times two are four does not mean the same thing to you as a believer and to someone else as an unbeliever. When you think of two times two as four, you connect this fact with numerical law. And when you connect this fact with numerical law, you must connect numerical law with all law. The question you face, then, is whether law exists in its own right or is an expression of the will and nature of God. Thus the fact that two times two are four enables you to implicate yourself more deeply into the nature and will of God. On the other hand, when an unbeliever says that two times two are four, he will also be led to connect this fact with the whole idea of law; but he will regard this law as independent of God. Thus the fact that two times two are four enables him, so he thinks, to get farther away from God. That fact will place the unbeliever before a whole sea of open possibilities in which he may seek to realize his life away from God. And it is this basic difference between what "two times two are four" means to the believer and what it means to the unbeliever that the doctrine of common grace has helped us to see. It has enabled us to focus our attention upon the antithesis without fearing that we are doing injustice to any of the facts that surround us.

Let us look then more fully at this antithesis and what it means for education. The first thing we would observe is that, if the universe to which the child is to be adjusted is thought of as impersonal, the one supreme result is that there are then no antitheses between the child and the universe. We may say, if we wish, that as Christian theists we have a life-and-world view in which the antitheses of life are not overlooked, while nontheists have a life-and-world view in which the antitheses of life are overlooked. For that reason every Christian knows that he cannot begin to build till he has first broken down, while every non-Christian thinks he can begin to build without any necessity of first breaking down.

Godless Education. Perhaps one of the most important points in this connection is to note that on the impersonalistic basis of our opponents there is no forensic relationship between man and his environment. How can anyone stand in a forensic relationship to an impersonal law? You cannot get any notion of what it might possibly mean that you should be legally responsible to law as such. Now the whole structure of Christian ethics or morality presupposes this forensic relationship. Scripture defines sin as a transgression of the law of God. Without the possibility and the actuality of a forensic relationship between God and man, the whole doctrine of sin falls by the board. And if sin falls by the board, the only thing that can be done with the evil in this world is to knit it into the constitution of the universe. Accordingly we find that both ancient and modern philosophy have maintained that negation is as fundamental as affirmation and that the devil is as old as God. Thus all ethical distinctions are reduced to metaphysical distinctions. "What ought to be is, and what is ought to be" is not merely the philosophy of certain philosophical schools but is the philosophy of all nonregenerate thought. And a consequence of this is that no Christianity is possible. There would be no sin and therefore no sin to remove. And if there were sin to remove, there would never be anyone able to remove it since it would be impossible that any one person appearing at any one point in the course of history should occupy the absolutely unique position that Christianity has attributed to Christ.

From these considerations it follows that if any ethics or morality is to be taught in schools that are based upon this impersonalistic philosophy, it must be pagan ethics or morality. So too if any religion is to be taught, it must be pagan religion. Everything that is truly Christian is in the nature of the case excluded.

In the second place the complete removal of all antitheses between the child and its surroundings appears still more fully in the fact that the impersonal conception of the universe has of necessity led to a complete relativism of all things. The "eternal ideas" of Plato did not for long remain eternal. Plato himself injected temporalism into them when he insisted on the ultimacy of evil. By doing this he made the ideal world dependent upon the temporal world. Time became a moving image of eternity. In modern days this motif has been worked out fully until Pragmatism openly avowed an exclusive temporalism, while Idealism made time and eternity correlatives with the "Concrete Universal." It could not have done otherwise. The impersonal means nothing if it is not related to the personal. If the impersonal cannot be related to and derive its meaning from the absolute personality of God, it will in the nature of the case be subjected to the personality of man. The evolutionary theory is only a particular manifestation of this general tendency. It is quite hopeless to fight evolution in the public schools and think that in doing so you have gone to the bottom of the trouble. Back of evolution lie relativism and impersonalism.

It will be seen at once that upon such a relativistic basis there can be no antithesis between man and his environment. On such a basis God and man are mutually dependent upon one another. And if you say that this very relativism provides for an infinity of antitheses, it is true in a sense; but in such a case there is no one to settle the antitheses, and they are thus rendered meaningless. Man does not stand higher than God and God does not stand higher than man. Who is to judge the other?

Humanistic Education. Now a Christian will recognize in this process of the history of philosophy the realization of the plans and purposes of Satan. The first thing he did for the human race was to tell Eve that nothing would happen to her if she ignored what she thought were the laws of God. He instilled into her mind the notion that the universe is neutral, that is, that there are no antitheses in it. The devil told Eve that he was just as old as God. The devil told Eve that there was an impersonal law above both

God and himself. He did not openly deny the personality of God. He implicitly denied the absolute personality of God. Satan is not opposed to personalistic philosophies. He can sometimes use them more effectively than outspoken impersonalistic philosophies when he wants to make non-Christians believe that they really are Christians.

Now when the educational curriculum of a school is based upon such a relativistic educational philosophy, the child is sure to learn that it really does not matter at all what he does. Oh yes, it does matter as far as getting through this life is concerned. It is still the best policy to be honest. Yet if you are dishonest, that too does not matter as long as you can "get away with it." The whole universe is then a place to "get away with" things. "The Lord doeth no good neither doeth He evil." [2] The "Lord" becomes but a symbolic expression for the impersonal laws of nature.

When Zephaniah the prophet noticed this sort of attitude getting into the lives of those who were Jehovah's covenant people, he preached the antithesis in its highest possible expression. He preached the judgment day as a day of wrath and of tribulation. God's people could not possibly insult their Maker and Redeemer in any more gruesome fashion than by having anything to do in their educational policies with those who said that God was dead. When God was no longer recognized either in his promises or his threats, the climax had been reached of all that the devil could possibly desire. To ignore God is to go to perdition without so much as a bump.

God-centered Education. It goes without saying, then, that our first duty as Christian educators is to face this education without antithesis and to take a thoroughly antithetical attitude toward it. Modern educational philosophy gruesomely insults our God and our Christ. How, then, do you expect to build anything positively Christian or theistic upon a foundation which is the negation of Christianity and theism? Here it appears that we must be negative before we can be positive. We must negate the negation entailed in the educational philosophy about us in order that thereafter we may be truly constructive. All your construction and all your synthesis that have failed to negate this negation of modern philosophy is itself negative and destructive. Here lies the antithesis in education.

The Non-Christian Idea of Mystery

And now to look at the same antithesis from the point of view of knowledge rather than from the point of view of reality, we must note that according to modern educational philosophy man is thrown entirely upon his own resources. This is but a natural concomitant of an impersonalist theory of reality. In an impersonal universe God can at the most be given the place of a collaborator with man in the field of knowledge. The void surrounds both God and man. Accordingly man makes himself the standard of truth. Nothing will happen to him if he thinks incorrectly about the nature of reality. Nothing will happen to him if he does not choose to think about the nature of reality at all. Says D. C. Macintosh, "There is no law human or divine to force man to waste his time on matters on which he feels no real concern; and since the human capacity for interest is limited at best it perhaps is just as well that he should keep to the things to which his special bent inclines him."[3] In Tolstoy's *Anna Karenina*, one of the main characters expresses it as his opinion that the gods will certainly not take it amiss of us if we have made some mistakes about them, inasmuch as we have done the best that we could. Now such a way of presentation presupposes that man has never had any contact with God and has never had any information about the truth of reality, which would make it an insult to God to think mistakenly about him and his universe.

And how does man feel now that he has for centuries tried for himself the task of interpreting reality without any reference to God? He has done his best. He has courageously entered the field with the crowbar of his intellect in order to conquer all mystery or, if you will, conquer *the* mystery. When his intellect failed him, he tried to descend into the lower levels of his existence in order to receive there some feeling of what it is all about. And when that failed, he was driven to the conclusion that reality is *essentially irrational*. That is the prevailing view today. We are told that a surd remains no matter how carefully and exhaustively we may study any particular fact.[4] And as for the notion that men can have knowledge about reality as a whole, it is said to be based upon conceit. The philosopher of today has given up every attempt to understand the meaning of the whole of reality. "The contemplation of total reality, the idea of knowing so as to understand what total reality, historically and in the present, might be, is a fundamental mistake; the existence of this total reality is itself open to question."[5] And yet the philosopher is also conscious of the fact that all things are related. He knows that unless we know the whole we cannot really know any part of the whole. The question of the one and the many is to him as insoluble as it was to Plato and Aristotle. The whole of reality is in darkness and consequently a surd surrounds every particular fact.

The net result of all this is that modern man feels himself adrift as a derelict on a shoreless sea. He is overwhelmed with a sense of the utter futility of it all. More than that, he feels terrified. He speaks much of

"Lebensangst" ("life-anxiety"). "Anxiety arises to the consciousness, as a lost point rises to be swallowed up in an empty expanse, since all human relationships are of only temporary value."[6] Man feels that he is somehow significantly related to that ultimate irrational existence about which he has no knowledge and over which he has no control.

Looking at this modern Irrationalism, what else can we do but reject it *in toto*? If we give to God his rightful place as absolute self-conscious personality, we have the very opposite of Irrationalism. In that case we know that our knowledge is analogical of God's knowledge and therefore true. We live and move and have our being in the revelation of God. And as for Scripture, it is then but the means of the reinstatement of man into the original revelational atmosphere in which he was created. We make no apologies for regarding Scripture as the textbook of the philosophy of science. Granted the existence of God and granted the existence of sin, the imperative necessity of redemptive revelation follows unless God should fail of his purpose with man. "If ye believe in God believe also in me," said Christ. As theism is the presupposition of Christianity, so Christianity is the implication of theism. We are in no doubt about either. Fear of the void is the controlling motive of the unbeliever's life. Confidence in God is the controlling motive of the believer's life. And you cannot be positive on a basis of fear. You cannot construct into the void, especially when you stand upon the void. Here again we must negate the negation entailed in modern education before we can really be constructive in anything that we do.

Uncertainty and Fear. And if now we turn to the educational picture that surrounds us, we find that it corresponds exactly to the educational philosophy that we have been discussing.

In the first place we would note the excited interest in matters educational. The number of books on education is legion. Man throws all his hopes on the education of the next generation. He is conscious of the fact that the present generation is in a hopeless condition. "A generation which has no confidence in itself occupies itself with education, as though here again something could come into being from nothing."[7]

In the second place there is no centrality in the educational policies of the day. How could there be if no one knows what the center of human life is? Instead of following a policy that is based upon a definite assurance that human life must be lived for the sake of God, we find a hasty and nervous series of experimentations into the unknown. One demagogue after another arises to proclaim: Lo, here is the Christ; and lo, there is the Christ. Since man thinks he has no knowledge of reality but at most a glimpse now and then as to what he may accomplish in this world, his educational policies are split up as to purpose, as to content, and as to method. Educational theorists are out of breath. They dash after one thing and then after another as dogs do after a ball that is carelessly thrown out. What else then can we do but negate this negation of a center and a goal in education?

As to the purpose of education we are told that it is to teach the growing personality a method of adjustment to the environment in which it may be placed. This purpose is set in opposition to what is said to be the older conception of the purpose of education, namely to give the child a certain informational content. Functional education is substituted for conceptual education. But if we look for a minute at this so-called functional theory of education we notice that it cannot possibly function. The reason for this is that nothing will function in the void. It is perfectly self-contradictory to say that the purpose of education is to teach people adjustment to environment if neither we nor anybody else can have any notion whatever as to what that environment may really be. There can be no preparation for the void. In trying to prepare for the void modern educational theory has missed all sense of direction.

In contrast to this we can readily see that only the Christian conception of education can really be said to be the functional conception of education. Upon a Christian basis there is assured a conviction as to what the growing personality will meet in the environment with which it will come into contact, and functional adjustment can be made accordingly. It becomes evident how absolutely imperative it is for any teacher who becomes enamored of the modern idea of functional education to ask himself whether such an idea of education is consistent with the Christianity that he professes. All too often have Trojan horses come into the Christian camp.

Knowledge and Confidence. The case is similar with respect to the content of Christian education. Here, too, we shall have to be increasingly fearless in letting the controlling concepts of the Christian-theistic life-and-world view determine what shall be the center of the curriculum. If we constantly keep looking over the fence to see how many hours are spent on this subject and how many hours are spent on that subject, we shall not get very far. If we are always worried about the criticism of our opponents, it is a sign that we have not yet learned the lesson to build alone. Again, this does not at all mean that we cannot learn from our opponents. During the World War the Germans no doubt learned from the Allies and the Allies learned from the Germans. Yet it is equally true that the Germans never failed to use what they learned from the Allies against the Allies and the Allies never failed to use what they learned from the Germans against the Germans. Thus, too, we can afford to take over from our enemies only that which will fit into our own program of constructing a covenant personality. No educational content that cannot be set into a definitely Christian-theistic pattern and be conducive to the development of covenant personality has any right to appear in our schools.

And finally this is also true of educational method. Here, too, the temptation besets us that we should be very keen to watch the methods that are used around us. Now this too is in itself altogether commendable and necessary. It is commendable because every good soldier should know the tactics of the enemy. It is commendable too because perhaps some of the methods used by the enemy may be transformed and used by us. But *transformed* they must always be. We cannot afford to say that if only we place a different content before our pupils we need not worry about the form because the form is neutral. If a glass has contained carbolic acid you do not merely pour it out in order then to give your child a drink of water. How much more impossible will it be to take a non-Christian spiritual content and pour it out of its form in order to use the latter for the pouring out of a definite Christian-theistic content? The connection between form and matter is too much like that of skin and flesh to allow for the easy removal of the one without taking something of the other. It is incumbent on us to be on our guard with respect to the educational methods of our opponents. We can never, strictly speaking, use their methods. We can use methods that appear similar to theirs, but never can we use methods that are the same as theirs.

So, then, our conclusion with respect to the educational philosophies and the educational policies that surround us is that we must be intensively and extensively negative or we can never be intensively and extensively positive in the Christian-theistic sense of the term. The fundamental principle of the antithesis upon which Christianity is built demands nothing less than that. We must more and more dare to be consistently peculiar in our educational policies. If we dare to be peculiar we will be "peculiar" in the eyes of the world, to be sure, but we will not be "peculiar" in the eyes of God. If we are not peculiar, we will be "peculiar" in the eyes of God and be twice "peculiar" in the eyes of the world.

II. The Antithesis in the Curriculum

And now, if you will speculate with me a little, I would like to look at some of the features that, it would seem, should always characterize the curriculum of a Christian school. I purposely say that I wish only to look at some of the features that should never be missing. I do not presume to lay down a program.

In order to consider the curriculum in its broad outlines and not to lose ourselves in details, we may say that it deals with nature and history. It deals with "facts" of space and with "facts" of time. It matters not what subject you teach; whether it be mathematics, sewing, cooking, or music, you are dealing with *space-time* "facts." I speak of space-time "facts" even in preference to "facts" of space and time in order still further to simplify and centralize the question. All "facts" are inextricably interwoven with space and with time. We cannot intelligibly think of "facts" without thinking them in space and time. We may speak of space and time, if we will, as the form of the "facts" if only we recall that form and content too are inseparable. Empty space and empty time are meaningless concepts. We may say then that the curriculum deals with "space-time facts."

One more preliminary point we would make in this connection. A sharp distinction is usually made between "facts" and "laws." It is taken for granted that you have explained the "facts" if you have referred them to the "laws" according to which they work. But this is misleading. Laws are nothing but ways in which "space-time facts" behave. It is therefore more to the point to say that laws are aspects of the "facts" or are themselves a part of the larger "fact" that we are seeking to learn about the "facts." An historical "fact" is perfectly meaningless unless seen in the relation it sustains to all other historical "facts," or in other words unless seen according to the law of its operation. So, then, for our purposes it is better to include the term "law" under the term "fact." The phrase "space-time facts" would then include all the "facts" and all the "laws" in their concrete relationship.

And now with the consideration of these preliminary matters we have also prepared the way for a direct attack upon the problem as to what would be the main feature of any Christian school curriculum. This main feature, it would now appear, is that the whole of "space-time facts" should be set into the pattern of the conception of the absolute personality of God.

The Non-Christian's Self-Sufficiency

We have seen that a "fact" without its relation to space is to us without significance. It is unintelligible. It is a mere abstraction. It is wholly unthinkable. And for these reasons it is *altogether unteachable.*

Similarly a "fact" in space without time is a mere abstraction and unteachable. You cannot tell anyone anything about such a thing because it does not mean anything to yourself. And it seems still to be a requirement that he who tries to teach should at least have some remote notion as to what it is all about.

Teaching Without Reference to God. Now, just in this way the whole of "space-time facts" is to a Christian a mere abstraction, wholly unintelligible and therefore altogether unteachable unless it be seen in its relationship to God as its presupposition. We may express the same idea by saying that no "fact" is seen as it really is unless it is seen in its correct relationship to God. Since God has made the space-time facts, their relation to God is naturally the most important thing to know about them. But more than that, it is not really enough to say that the most important thing to know about a "fact" is its relationship to God because that very relationship to God exhausts the meaning of the fact. When you have seen the "space-time facts" in their relationship to God, you have for the first time seen the *fact* about the "facts"; that is, you have for the first time seen the *facts* in distinction from bare facts. Accordingly, anyone who does not see the space-time facts before the background or in the pattern of the absolute personality of God does not see any facts but only thinks he does. It is not true to say that everybody has the facts to begin with. On the contrary, only a Christian theist has the facts because there are none but theistic facts. In one sense, we could of course say that all men "have" the facts, since all live in God's created order and all move in the general revelation of God. But the nontheist refuses to acknowledge the Creator who alone can be the proper context for interpreting any fact. Therefore nontheists deal only with "bare facts," that is, with abstractions that have no meaning.

We are purposely bringing the matter to this irreducible level in order to get away from the dangerously misleading confusion that appears perhaps more glaringly in the educational field than anywhere else, namely, that a fact is a fact for everybody alike, unbeliever as well as believer. Now this is either a truism or a satanic falsehood. It is a simple truism if we mean that Christianity is either true or it is not true. If it is true, then this truth does as a matter of fact exist for the unbeliever as well as for the believer, and the unbeliever will learn to know the facts when it is too late, as the parable of the rich man and Lazarus teaches us. But it is a satanic falsehood to say that a fact is a fact for everybody alike, if it is taken to mean, as it is usually taken to mean, that there is a realm of space-time fact that is known to all men alike. The whole point in dispute between a theistic and a nontheistic interpretation of reality is this question, whether "facts" can be facts without being theistic. It follows then that to say that the facts are facts without saying anything further is to give yourself over soul and body to the mercy of your enemy, who likes nothing better than that you should give up the battle before the first blow has been given. As theists our contention is that there are no facts but theistic facts, while the contention of our opponents, expressed or unexpressed, is that facts are facts whether God exists or does not exist. For us to admit this at the outset would be complete admission of defeat and would spell utter bankruptcy as well as the uselessness of Christian education.

Teaching With Reference to God. What sense is there in spending money for teaching arithmetic in a Christian school rather than in a so-called neutral school unless you are basically convinced that no space-time fact can be talked about and taught unless seen in its relationship to God? When speaking thus of the absolute antithesis that underlies the educational policies of our schools, it is not too much to say that if any subject could be taught elsewhere than in a Christian school, there would be no reason for having Christian schools. The only reason why we are justified in having Christian schools is that we are convinced that outside of a Christian-theistic atmosphere there can be no more than an empty process of one abstraction teaching abstractness to other abstractions. No teaching of any sort is possible except in Christian schools.

No, please do not say that this is an extreme statement or an overwrought accusation. Plato knew it and said so. He knew that he could do nothing with the profound notion that two times two are four if he looked at two horses and two cows. He found that he would somehow have to make a reference to the ideal world and speak of two-ness abstracted from horses and cows and everything concrete. But two-ness—what was it? Plato knew that he did not know. He knew that the ideal world was not within his grasp. But he also knew that he was helpless without it. And this was true with respect to everything that he saw in this world. It was true of mathematics but it was also true of ethics. Can virtue be taught? he asked. Well, to teach a thing we must know that thing. But do we know virtue by looking at it in this world? No, for there is no virtue here that is not mixed with vice. Any virtue driven to extremes becomes a vice. To get a true idea of virtue, then, we must look at the ideal world again. But even there we cannot find virtue totally by itself because among the ideas of good things there are those terrible ideas of mud and hair and filth. In the ideal world, too, Plato thought the positive does not exist without the negative, the devil is just as old as God. So then the idea of virtue as Plato saw it remained an ultimate mystery. Plato admitted that he was before an ultimate dilemma of thought. He knew that he knew nothing and that he could therefore teach nothing.

As for modern philosophy, it knows still better than Plato did that it knows nothing, but the pity is that it is not willing to admit as Plato was willing to admit that it cannot teach anything. Bernard Bosanquet has labored to understand what it means that five plus seven are twelve. He calls it an eternal *novelty*. He also calls it an *eternal* novelty. By that he means that no law of arithmetic means anything to anybody unless such a law is related to a body of absolute truth. His argument was the same as Plato's when he said that to know what it means that two times two are four we must know what two-ness means. Now here we have a full admission of the indispensability of Christian schools. The ground for the necessity of Christian schools lies in this very thing, that no fact can be known unless it be known in its relationship to God. And once this point is clearly seen, the doubt as to the value of teaching arithmetic in Christian schools falls out of the picture. Of course arithmetic must be taught in a Christian school. It cannot be taught anywhere else.

Consciousness of Antitheses

We have purposely taken up this matter of two times two are four because that seems to be the black beast in Christian instruction. Many are willing to admit that it is quite reasonable that the Christian religion and Christian ethics should be taught in Christian schools but are not willing to admit that subjects which lie on the educational periphery should be taught in Christian schools. The most they will admit is that of course it is nice to have the children in a Christian atmosphere at all times and that such a Christian atmosphere can be supplied by Christian teachers only. Sometimes some say sneeringly or at least doubtfully, "How can you be specifically Christian when you teach the children that two times two are four?" Well, our answer is that if you cannot teach arithmetic to the glory of God, you cannot do it any other way because it cannot be done any other way by anybody. And by this I do not mean that you have breathed a sort of Christian atmosphere about the problems of arithmetic in the sense that you have opened the school session with prayer a couple of hours before. By a Christian atmosphere I mean first of all that deep conviction on the part of the teacher that no fact is teachable except when brought into relationship with God. For it is not till the teacher has this conviction that he will radiate any ethical atmosphere that is worth the having. Emotional Christianity does not flower well on a hard clay bottom of intellectual paganism.

Now, I well know that it is easy to figure this thing out in theory and most difficult to bring it into practice. Ah, how large a portion of the grace of God it requires to be a teacher of the children of the covenant! But do we not sometimes too lightly dismiss the matter as beyond our power altogether? When we say that arithmetic must be taught to the glory of God we do not mean that the child shall at once understand the full implication of all that it means that two times two are four because God has made the space-time world according to certain laws and that these laws express something of the very being of God. We need not at all despair when the first grades do not understand this matter. But you may as well despair if your eighth or tenth graders do not begin to get an inkling of it. They ought to begin to see these things, and if they do they will later learn to see more of them.

Then, too, there is a sense in which the subject of arithmetic lies at the periphery of the Christian school curriculum. Not as though arithmetic should take less time than other subjects. It is quite possible that a subject should take a large share of the available time and yet lie at the periphery of the curriculum. Arithmetic and all other subjects that emphasize the space aspect of the space-time world lie in the nature of the case at the periphery of the whole area of the creation of God. This is due to the arrangement God has made in his creation, namely, that man should stand at the center of it. And since man is a self-conscious and active being, his most characteristic human traits will manifest themselves more fully in the movement of time, that is in history, than in the immovable atmosphere of space. Accordingly it is easier to bring out the more specifically human and the more specifically Christian interpretation of reality when teaching history than when teaching nature. Consequently, we cannot expect the same intensity of emotional response to a really Christian instruction of arithmetic that we can expect to a Christian instruction of history. And for that reason, too, we should again realize the close connection between the facts of space and the facts of time. Since the more definitely temporal facts lie closer to the center of the glory of God, we should connect the spatial facts with the temporal facts and use the latter as media of transmission of the glory of the spatial facts to God. In a symphony every individual instrument need not be individually conspicuous. In a good picture there is much background that is little noted but nonetheless indispensable. The curriculum of a Christian school should be an organism in which some members seem less important but cannot be amputated.

Let me interject again that when I have maintained that no teaching is possible except in Christian schools, I have not forgotten the doctrine of common grace. Of course in a non-Christian context arithmetic (and for that matter everything else, including religion and Christianity) is teachable if by being teachable you mean nothing more than making susceptible to a temporary pragmatic manipulation by unbelievers. But we are not speaking of that now. We are speaking only of specifically Christian instruction and of absolutely ultimate matters.

The Natural Precedes the Spiritual. While speaking of the curriculum we have emphasized the all-important point that every space-time fact must be set before the absolute personality of God because we feel that, if this point is once clearly seen, all other problems can be solved in the light of it. We cannot speak of many of these problems. Let us, however, look for a moment at this question of centrality in the curriculum on which we have already touched. It goes without saying that if there is centrality in our Christian life-and-world view, there is of necessity also centrality in our educational curriculum. We have spoken of the lack of centrality in the educational *policies* that surround us and found that such a lack of centrality was due to the lack of centrality in the educational *philosophy* that surrounds us. So also there is a lack of centrality in the *curricula* of the schools that surround us. It could not be otherwise. No one can make a curriculum that has a center if he has no center for his own life-and-world views.

We are all familiar with the mad rush for the study of nature at the expense of the classics and the humanities a number of years ago. Now we are not interested in the details of this question. We only wish to point out that this tendency was indicative of an emphasis upon man's environment at the expense of man himself. And if now we recall that according to modern educational philosophy man does after all know nothing about his environment, it becomes apparent that the modern educational curriculum is built upon the silent admission that we do not know who man is and that we do not know what his surroundings are. Accordingly man is wholly adrift, and all that he can do is to turn as fast as he can to anything that he may fancy himself to see in the distance.

The curriculum of a Christian school will naturally maintain the exact opposite of all this. We know who man is and what his surroundings are. Moreover we know that man is the center of the curriculum-building program. As builders of a curriculum for Christian schools, therefore, we do not dash wildly back and forth, first in this and then in that direction. We will always place man at the center of the curriculum. God has made man's environment subject to man instead of man subject to his environment. It follows that history can never be relegated to the background. It is in history that the acts of man appear most conspicuously. Note well, we are not speaking first of all of the quantity of time required to teach these subjects. Nature study is good and useful if only it is not separated from the study of history.

All Things Are Ours. But we have not said enough if we say that man must always be at the center of the curriculum. We must add that man as the Christian must stand at the center of the curriculum. Hence sacred history, which focuses on the program of redemption, is at the center of all the teaching of history. Again I speak not primarily of a quantity of time. To say that sacred history should stand at the center of the curriculum is not inconsistent with spending many hours on subjects other than sacred history. It means that only when nature is brought into connection with history and secular history is brought into connection with sacred history does man as redeemed stand at the center of the curriculum, and only thus can any and every fact of the space-time world be brought into relation with the absolute personality of God. Only thus is there no abstract separation of the *that* of education from the *what* of education. Only thus can teaching become really concrete. Only thus can the emphasis be laid where it ought to be laid. It will enable us to set forth the really important figures in the history of the human race and in the history of the redemption of the human race without being all the while afraid that we are spending too much time on Moses rather than on Mussolini. Only thus can nature be set forth as the picture book of God, that is, as the moving picture book of God. Only thus can we provide the atmosphere that is so indispensable if Christian education is to be worth its name.

III. The Antithesis in Regard to the Child

And now that we come to a consideration of the child that is to be educated, we can be very brief. We have already discussed what the modern educational philosophy thinks of man. It will naturally think the same thing of the child. Out of the maze of the void and out of the infinite depths of irrationality there has somehow come forth upon this world these specks of rationality that we call human beings. And each human being recapitulates this process of the race as a whole. The adjustments that the tiny speck of developing rationality must learn to make seem all to deal with temporal things, but there is a misty haze of possibilities surrounding him. Accordingly the child must be placed before an infinite series of open possibilities. The most common term used for this supposed process of adjustment is the phrase, the "integration of personality" into its surroundings. The concept of personality is used over and over again. The whole of education is said to be the development of personality. And it is said that only now that education is liberated from the trammels of medievalism, which made the child subject to the curriculum instead of the curriculum subject to the child, has personality any real chance for development.

The Non-Christian Idea of Personality

This question, then, of personality and the possibility of its development is the point in dispute between our opponents and ourselves. What shall we say in answer to the charge that in our type of curriculum personality cannot develop at all? It is clear that we are once more face to face with an ultimate alternative.

Vacuum-Fed Babies. When discussing the philosophies of education we saw that our opponents in the nature of the case think our position wholly untenable and that we think our opponents' position to involve nothing short of chaos. When discussing the curriculum we saw that the real issue was whether upon a nontheistic basis anything at all was teachable. And we have maintained that upon the educational foundation of our opponents nothing at all is teachable. That was our answer to the charge made by our opponents that we cannot teach because we are hide-bound in the formation of the curriculum. Our answer now to the charge that personality cannot well develop in our system of education can be nothing other than that on their system of education personality cannot develop at all. Here, as along the whole front, we must begin with an absolute negation before we can be positive and constructive at all.

Genuine Nurture. Our reason for holding that personality cannot develop in the educational system of our opponents is that on their view finite personality is, as we have seen, placed in the midst of an absolutely impersonal atmosphere. Our claim is that finite personality cannot develop unless it is placed face to face with absolute personality. We have contended that no space-time fact in general can have any significance except when placed in its proper relation to God. And personality is a space-time fact. But more specifically than that, the fact that nothing in this universe can be known except when placed into its relationship to God appears most clearly in the case of human personality. You cannot think of personality without thinking of rationality, and finite rationality is by itself unthinkable and without meaning. To think of finite personality by itself is to think meaning into the void. The impersonal cannot be a foil to the personal. Taken in an absolute sense personality must be completely self-sufficient. And taken in a finite sense, personality may have the impersonal as its foil only if back of this impersonal foil is the absolute personality of God.

It was the impersonalism of the non-Christian educational philosophies that reduced all antitheses to nothing and reduced the universe to a neutral universe in which nothing would happen. So now again it is this same ultimate impersonalism that reduces finite personality to nothing. Consequently, nothing will happen in the way of the development of personality. If, then, the finite personality is not placed face to face with God, and the "facts" about which the finite personality is to learn or the environment to which it is to be adjusted is not placed face to face with God, there cannot possibly be any fruitful contact between the subject and the object of knowledge. To have knowledge at all, both the knower and the known must be in contact with God. Only through God can the two be brought together.

The Non-Christian Denial of Authority

And this brings us finally to remark on the question of authority in education. The relation of one person teaching another brings out at once the question whether the one has any authority to present his interpretation as absolute truth. Is there any authority at all? Will not authority when exercised by one upon the other hamper the freedom of the other? Our opponents hold that strictly speaking authority and freedom are mutually exclusive. True, they will allow for the authority of the expert in the sense that one person knows a little more about the actual performance of the universe than another; but authority in the ultimate sense, that is authority in the juridical as well as the expert sense, they will not allow.

Expert Authority. Now we are not pleading for the substitution of juridical for expert authority. But what we do claim is that on the basis of our opponents there is no authority at all and that without authority no teaching is possible. That there is no authority on the basis of our opponents is clear from the fact that on their basis there is no knowledge at all. And if there is no knowledge possible, no expert knowledge is possible.

Real Authority. Authority is nothing but the placing of the absolute personality of God before the finite personality of man. It follows, then, that if nothing can be taught unless it is taught in relation to God, nothing can be taught unless it is taught with authority.

It is this that makes the position of the teacher so infinitely difficult and at the same time so infinitely valuable. On the basis of our opponents the position of the teacher is utterly hopeless. He knows that he knows nothing and that in spite of this fact he must teach. He knows that without authority he cannot teach and that there are no authorities to which he can appeal. He has to place the child before an infinite series of possibilities and pretend to be able to say something about the most advisable attitude to take with respect to those possibilities, and at the same time he has to admit that he knows nothing at all about those possibilities. And the result for the child is that he is not furnished with an atmosphere in which he can live and grow. In contrast with this the Christian teacher knows himself, knows the subject, and knows the child. He has the full assurance of the absolute fruitfulness of his work. He labors in the dawn of everlasting results.

2

BEING REFORMED IN OUR ATTITUDE TOWARD THE CHRISTIAN SCHOOL

LOUIS BERKHOF

As the years roll by and conditions change, the conviction is growing on us that we need the Christian school and need it very much. The Christian school has been a source of inestimable blessings for the Reformed people of the Netherlands and for the nation of which they are an important constituent. It has also been a boon for the Reformed circles in our land and may by the grace of God help us to contribute something worthwhile to the life of our nation. Experience taught us to appreciate this school. Other Christians have frequently congratulated us on its possession, described it as one of the mainstays of our churches, and exhorted us to guard, to continue, and to develop it. And however much many may decry it as adverse to the unity of our national life, it certainly points the way to the solution of a problem that is now weighing heavily on our public school system.

It is just because we regard the Christian school as a real blessing that we are so solicitous about it. We have been willing to finance it, even though we also had to pay our share for the maintenance of the public school. We resent the expression of opinions in our circles which might dampen the ardor for the Christian school and put it in jeopardy. We are anxious to see this school continue and to bless us with its fruits in the future as it has done in the past.

If our Christian school is to continue in the future, it is absolutely essential that we be thoroughly Reformed in our attitude to that school. This means that we must have a firm grasp of the fundamental principles that are basic to our school system. It means that we must be positively convinced of the necessity of these schools for our children. It means that we must not be half-hearted in praying and giving and working for the maintenance and the improvement of those schools. It means, too, that we must convince the coming generation of the absolute necessity of our

Christian schools, and must persuade them to sacrifice and to labor for their continued existence.

I. Secular Approaches to Education

Nationalism and Education

Let us begin by asking ourselves the question, What should determine our attitude to the Christian school, if we are truly Reformed? Shall we say that the spirit of nationalism in education, which asserted itself in many lands in the previous century, and which calls for "tax-supported, publicly controlled and directed, and non-sectarian common schools," ought to be the determining factor? If we are of that opinion, we shall reason somewhat as follows: The state is supremely interested in welding its citizenry into a unity, in developing a national spirit, a national character, a national sense of justice, etc. Its future welfare, inner strength, and prestige among the nations of the world depend on this. The development of such a truly national spirit can only be accomplished by the establishment and maintenance of a national school system, a system of free schools, offering equal opportunity to the rich and the poor, and patronized by all the people. The establishment and maintenance of such schools requires taxation, and their efficiency will correspond to the degree to which the people are compelled to send their children to them. Only the state with its sovereign power can tax the people and can make education compulsory. Hence it follows that only the state can establish and maintain an effective free school system. Our public schools, which are schools for the state, are necessarily also schools by the state. They do not lose sight of the interests of the individual or of society in general, but they are primarily interested in the welfare of the organized community, i.e., of the state, in the training of American citizens. And as loyal citizens of the state we ought to appreciate those schools, improve the opportunity they offer for our children, and zealously oppose all partisan schools, because they make for division rather than unity.

Now, it can hardly be said that this is a characteristically *Reformed* attitude. It clearly implies the adoption of a species of utilitarianism. It proceeds on the assumption that a general education of the people, permeated with a strong spirit of nationalism, is of paramount value for the state because it contributes to its unity, greatness, and strength, and to the happiness of the greatest number of its citizens. It takes for granted that this is true even when the education given is divorced from religion.

And because this is so, it is held that every citizen should seek this education for his children. But right at this point a good many questions clamor for answers. Is it true that a strong spirit of nationalism pure and simple is the greatest boon of the state? Is there not a great deal even in the present demand for an international consciousness that is more in harmony with the supreme religious and ethical ideal of humanity? Will not a nationalism *permeated with the spirit of true religion* prove to be the greatest blessing for the state and contribute most to the happiness of the people? Shall we say that the preferences of the state ought to determine our attitude? Would we act on that principle if the state should decide to introduce a state religion? We leave these questions for your consideration and pass on to another idea.

Evolutionary Psychology and Education

Shall we say with modern evolutionary pedagogy that the child is the standard and measure of all things in education, and that a study of the child ought to determine the requisite education? Should such a study also be the determining factor in our attitude toward any school that makes a bid for the education of the child? If so, then we might reason somewhat along the following lines: The child reveals great similarity with the higher animals and is clearly a product of evolution. The animal origin of the child's mental make-up ought to be carefully considered, for this will point the way in his further education. There are many imperfections in the life of the child, but these do not constitute sin. They are merely manifestations of the lower animal propensities which are struggling for the mastery. The child is fundamentally good, however, and under proper conditions and wise guidance will naturally develop in the right direction. It is of the utmost importance that palatial school buildings be erected, surrounded by spacious and attractive playgrounds, that the halls be adorned with masterpieces of art, and that the classrooms be cheery and well ventilated. In any attempt to teach and guide the child, his needs, his desires, his will, and his rights should be carefully considered. He should not be taught that he is utterly corrupt and cannot in any case attain the ideal, but ought to be made conscious of the natural urge within himself to soar to the loftiest ethical heights, and of the inherent power to overcome evil and to rise to a state of moral perfection. He should never be constrained to learn things which are beyond his comprehension, such as religious mysteries and profound theological truths, but only what he can fully understand and assimilate. Above all, he should be left free to develop his own religion in harmony with the teachings of science, and should not be urged to accept the myths of the Bible, however beautiful they may be, nor to believe the Hebrew conception of creation and providence, of angels and devils, of sin and atonement, of heaven and hell.

Now if we adopt that position and reason along those lines, we shall hardly be enthusiastic supporters of our Christian schools. But again we remind ourselves of the fact that it is not Reformed to say that psychology, that the study of the child, must ultimately determine our attitude to the school in which the child is educated. Moreover, the study of the child does not necessarily lead to the view indicated in the preceding paragraph, however common this may be in the present day. And even if it did, it would only represent the result to which man with his darkened understanding, subject to the power of error and deception, came in reading God's general revelation, a revelation which, while it is sufficient to leave man without excuse, is nevertheless obscured by sin and has ceased to be a perfect reflection of the truth. It is only in the light of Scripture that we can give a true interpretation of God's revelation in nature, and it is therefore to the Bible that we must turn for guidance.

II. The Reformed Perspective on Education

If we are truly Reformed, we shall say that the will of God should determine our attitude to the Christian school, and that this will is revealed to us in his general, but above all in his special revelation.

Parents and Education

God has made known to us whom he regards *as the responsible educators of the child.* He has indicated this in his general revelation in nature in the orders which he has established. In the animal world he shows us how the old provide for their young, how they protect them and train them. We see the eagle fluttering over her young, exciting them to fly, hovering over them for protection, and carrying them when they are wearied; we see the hen gathering her brood under her wings. Jeremiah even holds up the jackal as an example for Israel, when he says, "Even the jackals draw out the breast, they give suck to their young ones: the daughter of my people is become cruel, like the ostriches in the wilderness" (Lam. 4:3). The gentile world hit upon the idea of parental obligation in the work of education. It is true that Plato wanted the state to take charge of this work, but his ideal state existed only on paper. Athens placed the responsibility for the work of education squarely on the family; all its schools were private schools. And of the five rights of the Roman citizens, that of the father over his children was the very first. He took great personal interest in the education of his sons. The home rather than the school was the center of the educational system. And even with respect to the school Pliny the younger expressed the opinion that the principle, "the school belongs to the parents," was the only sound principle. It should not surprise us that even heathen people without the light of special revelation saw that the parents were the proper responsible educators of their children, for nature itself points the way. The children are born of the parents and therefore belong to them first of all. The parents have them under their care until they set out on their own, and the parents are prompted by their parental love to provide for their children's physical, mental, moral, and spiritual needs. They guide them, protect them, and promote their best interests. There is no one interested in their welfare as much as their parents are. Hence it is but natural that the parents should be the responsible educators, and that, if the parents should feel constrained to call in the help of others, these others should feel that they stand in *loco parentis* (in the place of the parents, *ed.*).

God's special revelation teaches us the same truth with even greater clarity. Negatively, it may be said that the Bible in speaking of the duties of the state never mentions the work of educating the children of the nation (cf. Exod. 18:22-26; Deut. 1:16, 17; Matt. 22:17-21; Rom. 13:1-7; I Pet. 2:13-15). It is a striking fact that even the Old Testament, in which God deals with the nation of Israel more than with the individuals that belong to it and consequently speaks primarily in national terms, always refers to or addresses the parents as the responsible educators of the children. The book of Deuteronomy, the book of Proverbs, and Psalm 78 are very instructive in this respect. In the New Testament it is clearly indicated that the government must guard the interests of all those that belong to its realm, must judge between a man and his neighbor, must preserve order by punishing evildoers, and must levy taxes for the support of its work (Rom. 13:1-7). But when it speaks of the education of the children, it turns to the parents in the words, "Ye fathers, provoke not your children to wrath: but nurture them in the chastening and admonition of the Lord" (Eph. 6:4).

The Religious Character of Education

The Word of God also indicates very explicitly that the education which the parents are in duty bound to provide for their children *must be fundamentally religious.* In fact, its emphasis is so exclusively on religious training that it almost seems as if it regarded this as the whole of education.

This finds its explanation in the fact that Scripture deals primarily with the religious and moral needs of man, that it regards religion as the most fundamental, the most basic thing in the life of man, and that it would not consider any education as sound and satisfactory that was not permeated with the spirit of religion. Let us notice a few passages that bear on this point. In Genesis 18:19 we find God saying with respect to Abraham, "For I have known him, to the end that he may command his children and his household after him, that they may keep the way of Jehovah to the end that Jehovah may bring upon Abraham that which He has spoken of him." In these words we are informed respecting the reason why God decided to give Abraham an insight into his counsel concerning the coming destruction of the cities of the plain. Abraham was chosen by God to be the father of a mighty nation and a blessing for all the nations of the world. But in order that the promises to Abraham might be fulfilled and the Lord might really bring upon him the promised blessings, Abraham would have to teach his descendants "to keep the way of Jehovah, to do righteousness and justice." And in order that he might be a truly effective teacher of the great lesson that the blessings of Jehovah are enjoyed only in the way of obedience, and that the way of disobedience spells death, it had to be revealed to him that the cities of the plain were about to be destroyed for want of justice and righteousness. The book of Deuteronomy is shot through with exhortations to the Israelites to be diligent in reminding their children of the wonderful way in which God had led the nation in the past in order that these children might serve Jehovah with willing hearts. And we hear what may be regarded as the jubilant answer of the pious Israelite to all these exhortations in the words of the poet:

> I will open my mouth in a parable:
> I will utter dark sayings of old,
> Which we have heard and known,
> And our fathers have told us.
> We will not hide them from their children,
> Telling to the generation to come the praises of Jehovah,
> And His strength, and His wondrous works that He hath done.
> For He established a testimony in Jacob,
> And appointed a law in Israel,
> Which He commanded our fathers,
> That they should make them known to their children;
> That the generation to come might know them, even the children that should be born;

Who should arise and tell them to their children,
That they might set their hope in God,
And not forget the works of God,
But keep His commandments (Ps. 78:2-7).

It is that type of education that is pregnant with the promise of real blessings. If Abraham diligently teaches his children the way of the Lord, then the Lord will bring upon Abraham and his descendants the things which he has promised them. Listen to the words of divine wisdom: "Train up a child in the way he should go"—mark well, not "in the way he *would* go," but "in the way he *should* go," and this, according to teachings of Scripture, is the way of the covenant—"and even when he is old he will not depart from it" (Prov. 22:6). It is no wonder, therefore, that the New speaks in the same vein as the Old, exhorting the parents to educate their children religiously: "Ye fathers, provoke not your children to wrath; but nurture them in the chastening and admonition of the Lord" (Eph. 6:4).

The Child's True Nature and Education

This emphasis on religious education is exactly what we would expect in view of what the Bible reveals respecting the essential nature of the child. It is often said that man is incurably religious. Moreover, missionaries and students of comparative religion inform us that never a tribe was found without religion. The import of this is that the idea of God cannot be eradicated from the human soul. And this is impossible because man is God's offspring, the image-bearer of the Most High, everywhere and always. To separate the image of God from man is to rob him of his humanity. The image of God is the most fundamental thing in humanity generally, and consequently also in the child specifically. And that which is most essential in the child cannot be ignored in its education without doing injustice to both the child and its Creator and without turning its education into perversion. It is true that man by sin lost those moral and spiritual qualities that constitute the image of God in the more restricted sense, but this does not mean that he has ceased to be the image-bearer of God. He is still a rational and moral being, able to distinguish between good and evil; he still shows a certain appreciation of what is true and good and beautiful; and he still has a certain sense of the divine and an urge within him to engage in religious exercises. Moreover, we must bear in mind that the Spirit of God is operative in covenant children—I do not say, in every covenant child—and is restoring the image of God that was lost by sin. Therefore, Christian parents have an added reason to look upon their children as image-bearers of God.

The Unity of Education

Now sound psychology and pedagogy teach us that we must take that which is most fundamental in the life of the child into consideration *in the whole of his education.* There is a strong tendency in present-day psychology to emphasize the fact that the soul of man is a unit, acts as a unit, and consequently also reacts as a unit to all external influences, though it may manifest its action in a variety of ways. The old doctrine of the separate powers of the soul is not popular today. We are constantly reminded of the fact that it is the whole man that perceives and thinks, that desires and wills. Consequently, his education should also be regarded as a unitary process. It is utter folly to think that you can inform the intellect without giving direction to the will, that you store the head with knowledge without affecting the emotions, the inclinations, the desires, and the aspirations of the heart. The training of the head and of the heart go together, and in both the fundamental fact that the child is the image-bearer of God must be a determining factor. Again, in view of the fact that education is and should be a unitary process, we understand the absolute absurdity of saying that the school is concerned only with the head and should limit itself to secular education, while the home and the church make provision for the heart by adding religious education. We should never forget that the education which the child receives in the school, though divorced from religion, is nevertheless an education of the entire child and is bound to make a deep impression on the heart.

These considerations naturally lead us on to another point that deserves emphasis. The soul is a unit and education is a unitary process, aiming at the development of man's essential nature into a harmonious life, full and rich and beautiful. But this end can never be attained, if the home and the church on the one hand, and the school on the other hand do not have the same conception of the essential nature of the child, and do not agree in the fundamentals of their teachings. How can an education that proceeds in part on the assumption that the child is the image-bearer of God and in part on the supposition that it bears the image of the animal, an education that is partly religious and partly irreligious, i.e., anti-religious, ever result in a life that is truly unified? It can only lead to one thing, and that is a divided life so strongly condemned by our Savior (Matt. 6:22, 23), a life with scattered energies and dissipated powers, swayed and torn by conflicting opinions, lacking in singleness of purpose, in stability and strength, and in that true joy that fills the soul which is consciously moving in the right direction. We are in perfect agreement with the Modernists on this point, the only difference being that, while we maintain that in the training of Christian children the education of the schools should fundamentally conform to the religious education of the home and of the church, they strenuously assert that the religious education of the home and of the church must be in conformity with the scientific teachings of the schools. To the oft-repeated complaint that many young people suffer shipwreck religiously in our colleges and universities and even seminaries, they simply answer that the Christian home and the Christian church are to blame, because they have not prepared their children and young people for the advanced views in religion that are now taught in the schools.

The Reformed Christian, who believes that the child is the image-bearer of God, naturally proceeds on the assumption that that most fundamental truth may not be ignored in any part of his education, *and especially not in his school education.* This fact may well be stressed in our day. In view of the fact that the influence of the Christian home is waning, and that the church can devote only a couple of hours a week to the religious training of its youth, the school is easily the most important educational agency of the present. Is it not the height of folly even from a purely educational point of view to let the most important agency in education ignore that which is most essential and most fundamental in the life of the child? And can Christian parents reasonably expect their children to be imbued with a spirit of true religion if they persist in sending them to a school where for twenty-four hours a week they are taught in a spirit that is fundamentally irreligious, if not positively anti-Christian? The answer can only be a decided negative. And experience will bear out the correctness of this answer. America is today reaping in its churches what it has sown in its schools. It has sown through the secularized schools, and it is reaping a purely naturalistic religion.

III. The Christian School and Education

Objections to the Christian School

In view of all that has been said, it ought not to be so difficult to determine what is a truly Reformed attitude to our Christian schools. We may begin by saying that a person who is really Reformed, i.e., who makes the will of God the law of his life, and who is guided in all the relations which he assumes and in all the activities in which he participates by Reformed principles, *cannot possibly assume an attitude of hostility to the Christian school without compromising his religious convictions.* It is true that we sometimes witness the strange phenomenon that persons who profess to be truly Reformed reveal a decided opposition to the Christian school. And if we inquire into the reasons for this hostility, these persons frequently resent the query and leave it for us to surmise the truth. Sometimes, however, they will answer, and then point to one of the three following reasons or to all three combined. (1) They tell us that public opinion is down on the Christian school, and that it is foolhardy to go contrary to the prevailing ideas of the day. Public opinion is, after all, as President Wilson said, "the mistress of the world." Chances are that they who speak after that fashion are more concerned about their popularity than about their religion. (2) Very often they create the impression that the great expense entailed in the maintenance of separate schools constitutes their great objection to the Christian school, though they are generally loath to give expression to this sentiment. Their love of money plays a great part in their opposition. They seem to rate the material things higher than the spiritual. (3) Again, we find them pleading their Americanism as a ground for their hostility to private schools. The public school is the school of the nation, and every loyal American should send his children there for their education. By taking this stand they stigmatize as disloyal citizens the thousands and millions of Roman Catholics and Lutherans who maintain their own parochial schools, and also that large number of wealthy Americans who prefer and establish private schools for their children; and they argue this in spite of the fact that the nation and the states do not require that all children shall attend the public school and have never officially taken the stand that the establishment and maintenance of parochial and private schools conflicts with true Americanism. Those who advance this argument would evidently revise the statement of Jesus respecting the necessity of seeking first the kingdom of God, and make it read, "Seek ye first America, and all other things will be added unto it." And if there were alongside of the many free churches in our land also an established church, they would undoubtedly feel conscience-bound to join the latter, irrespective of its fundamental tenets.

Now, surely, such considerations as these do not warrant Christian people in opposing schools that make it their business to educate children in the fear of the Lord. It is hard to see how any child of God can make himself believe that in waging war against schools for Christian instruction he is fighting the battle of the Lord.

Toleration of the Christian School

But let us consider a slightly different attitude. Many Christian people who send their own children to the public school grant us at once that they would not be justified in taking a hostile attitude to the Christian school. *They want to be tolerant.* While they prefer the state supported schools for their own children, they have no objection to those who insist on having their children educated in private schools. Sometimes they are even willing to contribute to the cause of the Christian school. They seem to regard it somewhat as a matter of indifference, whether they send their children to the Christian or to the public school. This is not altogether the case, however. Their attitude reflects the idea that one *ought* to send his children to the public school, but *may* send them to the Christian school.

Now, this is certainly not a Reformed position. The standard of duty on which this proceeds is certainly not that of the Word of God, but simply some utilitarian consideration, centering on the individual, or on society, or on the state. Before we assume any such attitude as that, we ought to prove that the Bible, which is our ultimate standard of life and practice, explicitly or by implication favors state education for our children, whereas it also permits, but merely permits, the parents to assume direct responsibility for the education of their children by establishing and maintaining their own private schools. We should be in a position to maintain that the Bible deems it best that the religious element be excluded from the greater part of the education of our children, though it also allows, but merely allows, that their school education should also be permeated with religion. Now I do not think that any Reformed Christian would be very keen on trying to prove either one of those propositions. No one who regards the Bible as the ultimate standard of faith and duty can proceed on the assumption that the Christian school is a matter of indifference. Much less can he entertain the notion that the secularized school, the school that is divorced from religion, deserves the preference.

Religious Instruction in the Public School?

But granted that all this is true, is it not possible to assume *a compromising attitude*? There are Reformed Christians who evidently proceed on the assumption that the education which their children receive in the schools may not be divorced from religion and need not necessarily be irreligious in the public school. They maintain that it is possible and permissible to include the religious element in the instruction that is given in the tax-supported schools of the state. Consequently, they do not regard the Christian school as an absolute necessity, except in localities in which the last vestige of religion is excluded from the public school. We readily see that in taking that position they assume the right to yield their parental prerogative in the education of their children, to pass their responsibilities on to the state, and to leave it to the state to determine how much and what kind of religious training their children shall receive. This is certainly not in harmony with the Reformed principle that the parents are the responsible educators of their children, and consequently have the right to determine and the duty to control the religious spirit in which their children are educated.

Some are inclined, however, to waive the principle that the school belongs to the parents provided the parents can rest assured that their children will be educated religiously. Did not the government of the Netherlands in the post-Reformation period establish and maintain the schools where the children of the nation were educated? Did not the great Synod of Dort recognize and honor the government as having authority in educational matters? And then too, have we not been told repeatedly that there would have been no school struggle in the Netherlands if it had not been for the secularization of the national school? All these questions may be answered in the affirmative. But the facts implied certainly do not prove that the principle that the parents are the responsible educators of the children—and should therefore be able to control the spirit of the education that is given in the schools—is not thoroughly scriptural and Reformed. A great deal might be said in explanation of the fact that this principle did not always control the educational praxis of our Reformed forebears.

But suppose that we leave it out of consideration for the present and face the question whether the public school can give the children the religious training on which Reformed parents must insist. We would anticipate *a priori* that it would be entirely out of the question that a state which has no established religion but guarantees equality and religious freedom to all its citizens, a state which claims absolute neutrality in religious matters, should teach any particular religion in its educational institutions. It would even seem that such a state could consistently do only one thing, i.e., exclude all religious instruction from its schools. This is exactly the condition that obtains in France, where, according to Payne,

"The French Revolution made appear for the first time, in all its definiteness, the conception of the lay state, of the state neutral among all creeds, independent of all ecclesiastical authorities, and free from all theological bias."[1] Our government has been moving in the same general direction, though it has not yet shaken off all vestiges of religion. Its Puritan traditions still make themselves felt, and in virtue of these some insist on calling the United States a Christian nation. It is perfectly evident, however, that the term so applied is shorn of its real significance. Batten correctly remarks that "a state does not become Christian when it incorporates the name of Christ in its constitution or opens the sessions of Congress with prayer; neither is a state Christian when certain theological ideas are embodied in its legislation and certain ecclesiastical functionaries dictate the policy of cabinets. In any real sense a state is Christian when it possesses the spirit of Christ and seeks certain great Christian ends in and through its life and service."[2] Because of this difference between the United States and France, the public school of our nation is not yet everywhere neutral in the sense and to the degree that the French public school is neutral. In some localities the public school has retained something of a religious character. At the same time authorities, when speaking of it in general terms, do not hesitate to speak of it as *the secularized school.*

But just how much religious teaching will be tolerated in the public school? Draper says in his work on *American Education* that religion is not barred from the schools, but sectarianism is; and this is a distinction that is met with repeatedly. The line is generally drawn at sectarianism or denominationalism. But, of course, even this is a rather uncertain line, since even the Bible has repeatedly been declared to be a sectarian book in official decisions and opinions. Payne expresses the opinion that "the genius of our institutions seems to require that our public school should be purely a lay institution, i.e., an institution divorced from religion." He quotes the authoritative work of Judge Cooley on *Constitutional Limitations* to the effect that "compulsory support, by taxation or otherwise, of religious instruction" is one of "those things which are not lawful under any of the American constitutions"; and that "not only is no one denomination to be favored at the expense of the rest, but all support of religious instruction must be entirely voluntary." From this Professor Payne concludes that "the American public school should not only be unsectarian, but should be absolutely neutral as to religious bias."[3]

In view of what has been said we may be sure that in the public school the teaching of the doctrine of election, of the total depravity of man, of his absolute dependence on the grace of God for salvation, of the limited nature of the atonement in Christ, of all doctrines which are specifically Reformed, is altogether out of the question. More than that, it is impossible to teach the doctrines of the Trinity, the deity of Christ, redemption by his atoning blood, the necessity of conversion, etc. Still further, it would not even be permissible to teach that Jesus is the Christ, the Messiah promised by the prophets, and that Christianity is the only true religion. In other words, the very heart must be taken out of religious instruction before it can be permitted in the public school. And surely it ought to be out of the question for any Reformed Christian to compromise on such a basis.

But perhaps some will say that they have been able to make the public school in their locality thoroughly Christian and even Reformed. I am not in a position to evaluate this contention. There may have been, and there may be today, cases in which this is actually done, though I doubt it very much. In connection with this point I will only make the following remarks: (1) The laws of the land, even where they permit or even require Bible reading in the public school, forbid that sectarian or denominational teaching should be given there. (2) The decisions handed down by the courts of several states and the opinions expressed by attorneys-general are all in harmony with the fundamental position that sectarian instruction must be absolutely excluded. I have yet to see the first verdict or opinion to the contrary. (3) According to Judge Cooley, certainly no mean authority, it is unlawful under any of the American constitutions to use the money that is raised by taxation for sectarian instruction. (4) In cases in which the school board of some country district succeeds in evading the law by introducing sectarian instruction, the complaint of a single individual will prove sufficient to put an end to its doubtful practice. And it would undoubtedly be rather embarrassing for a public school board made up of Christians to be called to account by one who is perhaps an unbeliever. (5) We may be sure that the opportunity for such an evasion of the law will also decrease in the measure in which the district school is replaced by the town school. And the tendency at present is rather strongly in that direction. In view of all this it appears that the practice of introducing sectarian instruction into the public school is very questionable, both from a legal and from a moral point of view. They who engage in it are using money, raised by taxation, for sectarian purposes, and this is contrary to the law. They introduce denominational teachings into the public school in spite of the fact that this is explicitly forbidden. They surreptitiously employ a state institution for the dissemination of specific religious doctrines. Surely, the foundation on which they are building is a questionable and a precarious one. It is a foundation that may crumble at any moment, a foundation that is "sinking sand." And one who is truly Reformed cannot consistently build on such a foundation in the important task of the religious education of his children.

Religious Instruction in Home and Church

Shall we then say that the home, the catechism class, and the Sunday school can take care of the religious training of the child, and that the school need not be burdened with this in any way? This position has been taken by many in the past, but the fallacy of it is becoming ever increasingly apparent. Educational reformers are proclaiming from the house tops that our educational system has not provided sufficiently for the religious training of our youth. Psychologists are reminding us of the fact that education is a unitary process. And if this is so, it is sheer folly that the most important educational agency of the present should neglect the most fundamental element in education; and also that the education of the school should be diametrically opposed in spirit to that of the Christian home, because this is bound to result in a divided life. Moreover, the many plans that are devised for the injection of a larger amount of religious education into the training of youth all testify to the insufficiency of the religious education of the last half century. And, unfortunately, they themselves are only halfway measures, which do not help us to escape from the dualism that now exists between the education of the public school and that of the Christian home.

Conclusion

If we allow ourselves to be controlled by the will of our God and by thoroughly Reformed principles in providing for the education of our children, we shall seek, wherever this is possible, to establish and maintain schools which will consider it a sacred duty to educate our children in the spirit in which we solemnly promised to have them educated. And if we find such schools already in existence, we will thank our God for them, we will love them, we will send our children to them. We will pray for them, work for them, and be ready to sacrifice for them. If in that spirit we and our children continue to labor for the cause of Christian instruction, we shall have the satisfaction of an approving conscience; we shall confer an inestimable boon upon our children, keeping them from the curse of the divided life and instilling into their hearts and minds ideas and ideals that are truly Christian; we shall make an important contribution to the spiritual welfare of our community and nation by depositing a seed that may yield thirty-, sixty-, and even a hundred-fold. Finally, we shall above all reap the blessing of our covenant God, who has promised that "our sons shall be as plants grown up in their youth, and our daughters as cornerstones hewn after the fashion of a palace" (Ps. 144:12).

PART TWO:
THE DOCTRINAL FOUNDATIONS OF CHRISTIAN EDUCATION

3

CREATION: THE EDUCATION OF MAN— A DIVINELY ORDAINED NEED

CORNELIUS VAN TIL

There is perhaps no concept underlying our system of education better fitted to bring out the distinctive character of Christian education than the concept of creation. Of course, it is not as though our concept of creation is the most basic concept of our system of education; the most basic concept of all is our concept of God. But our notion of creation affords a more readily available testing point than the notion of God. Creation has more directly to do with ourselves. It has to do with the universe that is visible. And as such it offers a ready target of attack for the enemy. The attacks on creation have been more direct and more self-conscious than the attacks on God. If one defends the notion of creation, he is directly regarded as defending something that very few will defend today.

Again, when the creation idea is seen to be the presupposition of the covenant idea, it brings out the distinctiveness of the *Reformed* view of education. There are many who, believing the Bible from cover to cover, also believe in creation. They are even quite ready to defend the creation idea against the evolution idea. Yet their fight is often in the interest of soteriology only. They know that salvation through Christ presupposes creation by God. But they see no need of fighting for the creation concept in order to assure a foundation for a genuine Christian culture. Since they have no eye for the meaning of the covenant, their interest in maintaining the biblical idea of creation is unbiblically narrow. Accordingly, as a corrective to this narrowly evangelical tendency we must defend creation as the very presupposition of the covenant. Only then will it bring out and give a foundation to the distinctiveness of our Reformed system of covenant education.

Now, we are to find in the idea of creation a divine ordinance for education. An ordinance for Christian education we usually seek and find in direct commandments of God to his people as they are recorded in the Scriptures. Or, more basically, we see such an ordinance to be involved in the covenant idea. Now, if possible more basically again, we are to find such an ordinance in the very notion of creation. And this is the right order of seeking for an ordinance of God for education. Direct commandments of God with respect to education are really no more than explications of the covenant idea. And the covenant idea is but a compressed statement of the educational principle involved in the idea of creation. When thus the direct commands of God are seen to be based upon the covenant and the covenant is seen to be based upon creation, there will be a proportionate increase in the conviction of the justice and necessity of our educational program.

But what, then, do we mean by education? *Education is implication into God's interpretation.* No narrow intellectualism is implied in this definition. To think God's thoughts after him, to dedicate the universe to its Maker, and to be the vice-gerent of the Ruler of all things: this is man's task. Man is prophet, priest, and king. It is this view of education that is involved in and demanded by the idea of creation.

It may be charged that we are at the outset arbitrarily setting up a certain theory of education and a certain theory of creation and then mechanically patching them together. Now, we would not only grant but also strongly affirm that certain theories of creation and certain theories of education stand or fall together. One of our chief interests is to see clearly this very fact. All too loosely are the terms creation and education bandied about. In the mouths of different men these terms may have any of several mutually exclusive connotations. We must know definitely what we mean by creation, what we mean by education, and why a certain view of education is involved in a certain view of creation. And then as to the charge of starting dogmatically we would only urge that this charge itself is based upon the dogmatically assumed position of neutrality. If the charge of dogmatism is to be hurled at us before we fairly get under way, we reserve the school-boy's right to say, "You did it, too." Perhaps neither of us can be neutral. At any rate, we state baldly first and defend afterwards.

Our method will, in fact, be purposely apologetic. That Christian instruction is based upon the Scriptures we know. That Christian instruction is involved in the covenant idea we also know. That Christian instruction is involved in the idea of creation we also, though perhaps less clearly, understand. But to defend Christian instruction against those of the contrary opinion is no easy task. Perhaps it will be a somewhat easier task if we see more clearly the relation between Christian education and the notion of creation. Perhaps we have tried to justify our educational policy by pointing to its fruits. But these fruits are not always the best. Moreover, you can point to external things and things for this life only. Perhaps we are hastily trying to improve our buildings and general technique in order to come up to public educational standards. But that race is hopeless and again pertains to externals alone. The final apologetic for Christian education must show that Christian education is involved in the covenant, that the covenant is involved in creation, that creation is involved in the idea of God, and that without God man's life and experience would be entirely meaningless. In the last analysis we need more than anything else an immovable assurance of the truth of the principle on which we base our educational policy. With this in mind we try to prove that whatever difficulties may be involved in our view of education, it is the only view that is reasonable for man to take.

We shall, in order to establish our position that in creation there is a divine ordinance for education, spend a large part of our time in reviewing the various philosophies of education in order to show that none of them, except the Christian-theistic philosophy of education, has any divine ordinance, in fact, any ordinance, any reason for its educational policy at all. Our contention will not be that there are no intellectual difficulties in our philosophy of education. There most surely are such difficulties. These difficulties are many and great. But there is no philosophy of education that has no difficulties. Hence it will not do, as was the easy custom of the rationalism of the eighteenth century, to cast the Christian theistic philosophy overboard because there were very patent intellectual difficulties involved in it. Nor, on the other hand, is it sufficient in order to defend the Christian-theistic philosophy of education to show that it has less, or at least, no more difficulties with which to contend than other philosophies of education. It is too late in the day of speculative thought for anyone to attempt to present a philosophy of education not well loaded with intellectual difficulties. The question is now one of to be or not to be. Is there any philosophy of education that can stand at all? Is there any such philosophy that does not reduce the whole of educational policy and procedure to a meaningless march from the inane to the void? We believe there is one and one only, namely, the Christian-theistic philosophy of education.

We do not now discuss how we have pedagogically received our view of education. Of course we have received it from parents and teachers, just as every human being receives his general philosophy from his forebears. But the question is, now that we have to assume the responsibility of educators, whether we would still continue to hold to that which we have received on authority when we were children. We would have to reject our views if the criticisms of others would make it clear to us that our views are unreasonable for a human being to hold. But if our investigation proves to us that it is unreasonable to hold to any other view, we are strengthened in the conviction of the reasonableness of our own.

Our apologetic can, accordingly, afford to use no time for details. There is often need for detailed apologetic, but detailed apologetic must always be fully conscious of its subordinate position. In the argument for and against organic evolution this is sometimes forgotten. The fight on this sector of the front is sometimes waged as though the issue could be settled by the data alone and once for all. So also men sometimes fight about the trustworthiness of the Scripture as though the next move of someone's spade in Palestine could determine everything. Facts, to be sure, are stubborn things, but facts must be interpreted. The philosophy assumed by evolutionists is a far more dangerous thing than the evidence that they bring. So also with the so-called facts of psychology and anthropology that have a bearing upon education. These facts, too, must be interpreted. And interpreted they are. Now all facts are interpreted in either of two ways. Men are either theists or anti-theists. The whole battle about facts is a mad scramble between these two kinds of philosophers. So every philosophy of education, too, is theistic or anti-theistic. It is on the major issue between theism and anti-theism that educational philosophies should meet.

The anti-theistic philosophy assumes myriad forms. Yet this multiformity should not deceive us. All forms of anti-theism reveal a common hatred for the theistic doctrine of creation. If a theism is theism indeed, with the notion of God as an absolute self-conscious personality as its determining concept, it can depend upon firm and persistent opposition from all varieties of anti-theism, however much they may propose organic union.

Thus the range and sweep of our apologetic for Christian education begins to assume form and shape. Our aim is to show that Christian education is based upon the notion of creation, that this notion of creation in turn is an inseparable part of the whole theistic philosophy of life, and that this philosophy of life is the most reasonable for man to take because all others reduce experience to something void of significance.

I. Christian Education Rooted in Creation

Our Christian education is based upon the notion of a temporal creation. There are many who incorporate the concept of creation into their system of thought but who mean by creation nothing more than logical dependence. Now, whatever creation may mean for someone else, for the Christian educator creation definitely implies that time and space do not exist in the same way for God as they exist for man. This fact will appear more clearly later. Suffice it here to indicate that here lies the pivotal point of difference between theists and anti-theists. Theism says that man is subject to the categories of space and time while God is not. Every variety of anti-theism says that space and time, if they are real, exist for God, if God is real, in the same way that they exist for man.

In the literature that deals with the problem of creation at all, such phrases as "the nature of thought" and "the nature of reality" recur again and again. The assumption of such statements is that *all* thought and *all* reality, whether divine or human, is subject to the same laws and limitations. Whether or not God can be personal is determined, for example, by asking whether thought, that is thought *per se*, can allow for the conception of absolute personality. That God cannot be absolute is sometimes deduced from the "fact" that all thought is relative. The only thing really known is that human thought is relative, but the assumption is made that divine thought must also be.

It is all-important to see that the opposition to the doctrine of creation and to theism in general is based upon this colossal assumption. If this assumption stands, the Christian schools must fall; but if this assumption falls, the Christian schools can stand.

If now one keeps clearly in mind this assumption of the identity of nature between human and divine thought, it will readily be understood why the idea of temporal creation must bear so much of the brunt of anti-theistic attack. Temporal creation implies the very denial of that assumption. Creation implies that God's thought alone is original and absolute, while human thought is derivative and finite. Creation implies that finite personality has been brought forth by absolute personality. Hence absolute personality could and did eternally exist in self-dependence with absolute self-interpretative power. Hence finite personality (man) would have to look up to absolute personality (God) as its pattern but could never set the ideal of absolute comprehension for itself. Finite personality must believe that complete, comprehensive interpretation exists in absolute personality and that this comprehensive interpretation of God furnishes the only basis for man's interpretation, as far as that interpretation goes. If one denies temporal creation, one must deny all that is implied in it.

The chief implication of temporal creation, the one most obnoxious to the anti-theistic assumption of the identity of the nature of all thought, is the implication that man can never claim intellectual comprehension as an ideal for himself. It is plain that if there is to be rationality anywhere there must be absolute rationality somewhere. If this were not so, rationality would float upon irrationality. If, then, human thought is identical in nature with divine thought, man must hold that complete comprehension of interpretation is a reasonable demand for him to make. If man's thoughts are not subject to greater limitations than God's thoughts, there is no reason why man should not eventually, if not now, understand all things; the unknowable is for him reduced to the unknown. Unless man makes the bold claim of essential comprehensibility for himself, he cannot be certain but that somewhere in the universe a God exists whose thoughts are self-dependent or absolute, and who will therefore shatter the very assumption on which man had made his claims. No god must be left who will be able to tell of the "slaughter of the gods."

Accordingly man *must* reject every view of creation that is not comprehensible to him. He must reject any view of creation that involves a qualitative difference between God and man. It is not the evidence offered in support of modern evolutionary theory that has brought the notion of special creation into disrespect; but it is the colossal assumption of all anti-theistic thought that has forced men, irrespective of facts, to deny the possibility of creation.

II. Anti-theistic Philosophies of Education

The argument most frequently used against the possibility of creation readily shows itself to be but the explication of the anti-theistic assumption just described. We are told that a God who was absolute or self-sufficient would not create the universe we are familiar with because he would have no need of it and it could have no meaning of its own. The only God that can possibly exist, now that this universe is here, is a finite God, and a finite God could not create the whole spatial-temporal universe. The argument restated runs thus: We cannot understand how a universe created by an absolute God can have meaning at all, and therefore no absolute God has created it. Or, our thought cannot exist independently of the spatial-temporal universe, hence an absolute God has not created it. The assumption of the argument clearly is that since our thought is not absolute, God's thought cannot be; God's thought must be identical in nature with ours.

But the attack on the creation doctrine has not always been so explicit. The conflict between theism and anti-theism has gradually become more self-conscious and outspoken. And an outspoken enemy is not the most dangerous enemy. It is the mask of friendliness toward the creation idea assumed by many anti-theistic philosophies that has always been and is now most dangerous of all. We must therefore trace some of the forms anti-theistic educational philosophy has taken in order to learn to recognize it even under cover.

Plato's Educational Philosophy

Plato's *Republic* is even today considered to be a classic of educational philosophy. No better illustration of anti-theistic education could be taken. His philosophy is typical. In his philosophy no attempt could yet be made to intertwine Christian and pagan motifs.

In Plato's philosophy there is, strange to say, an overemphasis on the timeless or eternal. Is this possible, judging from the theistic point of view? Yes, it is. Overemphasis on the eternity of God is impossible. But the overemphasis appears when man is made eternal as well as God. So Modernism today speaks much of the divinity of Christ, but also speaks of the divinity of man without realizing, unless it is dishonest, that it has thus necessarily changed the meaning of the term divinity when applied to Christ.

For Plato nothing is truly real unless it is eternal. The whole visible world is only faintly real insofar as it, somehow, partakes of the eternity of the invisible world of ideas. Man's soul is more real than his body because more of eternity dwells in the immaterial soul than could possibly dwell in the material body. Time itself is real insofar as it is a "moving image of eternity." And space as the matrix from which all visible things derive is itself somehow eternal.

It will appear that Plato has begun with the anti-theistic assumption of the identity of the nature of all thought, human and divine. His standard of reality is an abstract principle, a principle of thought *per se*, that is assumed to exist apart from God. God is real insofar as he can live up to this principle. The universe, at least the Ideal Universe, exists apart from God. God falls within the universe. Man, because somehow he partakes of this eternal principle, can determine all this with respect to God. It is this assumed rationalism that determines all of Plato's thought.

Some corollaries following from Plato's chief assumption we must note. In the first place principle is raised to a metaphysical status higher than that of personality. This elevation of principle above personality in the realm of reality must follow if one starts with an abstract principle in the field of thought or knowledge. God *must* be a dependent personality once the Platonic rationalism is one's starting point. Once abstract thought as a principle is accepted as the Umpire between God and man, God must be dependent because the Umpire must be higher than both God and man. Secondly, on the basis of the Platonic assumption one cannot speak of a temporal creation. God is within the universe, and the universe to be real must be eternal. It is this Platonic rationalism that has constantly been and is today the real source of opposition to the idea of temporal creation.

It is well that we see just what the Platonic conception of knowledge and reality implies for the interpretation of reality. In the Platonic philosophy interpretation becomes a cooperative enterprise between God and man. It is true that Plato honors God by lifting him to a rather high place in the universe. It is also true that Plato sometimes seeks in revelation for a solution of the problems with which he wrestles. But these facts do not qualify our statement that interpretation is for Plato no more than a cooperative affair. Man, though said to be created by God, has to be fashioned according to principles of goodness, truth, and beauty existing independently of God, out of material once more existing independently of God. Accordingly, man was really more dependent upon these abstract principles and the independent material than upon God. Thus man did not need to live by revelation only. He could live first of all by the embodiment of the principles of goodness, truth, and beauty; he could be a rationalist. He could, when unsuccessful in interpretation, ask God whether he, embracing somehow somewhat more of these principles, had any information on the matter in hand. But both God and man were dependent upon principles higher than themselves. Neither of them was the source of principle; both were embodiments of principle. There were areas of the unknown and unknowable for both God and man; they were wrestlers with Truth, both of them. Of course there could, on such a basis, be no divine ordinance for anything in the absolute sense of the term. There was no real authority of God over man. Both God and man needed education. One could really speak as well of a human ordinance for divine education as of a divine ordinance for human education.

Then, further, the cooperation between God and man may not be permanent. Cooperation of equals presupposes the independence of each member of the corporation. As long as all things go harmoniously, cooperation may continue. But is harmony, continued harmony, possible when there is a plurality of minds? It might be, we shall say, if both God and man were fully controlled by (because complete embodiments of the principles of goodness) truth and beauty. Sorry to say, these principles were not all-pervasive in the universe. They could not be in a world of space and time. Plurality itself involves evil for Plato because no member of the plurality can be comprehensive. There must be identity if there is to be harmony. Accordingly it could not be otherwise than that man must ofttimes differ from God on the matter of interpretation. And what could man do otherwise in such a case than follow his own honest convictions? Man, if rationalistic at the outset, must remain so to the end. Cooperative interpretation is really independent interpretation.

So man interprets reality for himself. He must even determine just what place God occupies in the universe. We may observe that Plato's view is identical with that of Eve in Paradise. Eve also elevated principles of right above God, and proceeded to determine for herself according to these principles what God's place was in the universe and what he could or could not do. Thus we learn to identify the Platonic assumption with the sin of man, the original and controlling sin of man. Thus we also understand what is meant by anti-theistic thought.

Anti-theistic thought, because of its initial assumption, *must* deny God. It *must* deny the possibility of the creation of perfect though finite beings. It *must* deny creation *per se*. It *must* deny the meaning of history if God exists. This is not because of difficulties involved in the theistic view of God—and the rejection of creation is the rejection of theism—but because it is assumed at the outset that theism is wrong.

Once this fact, that all of anti-theistic thought is based upon one colossal assumption, is clearly seen, we are not so easily tempted to yield to its siren song of open-mindedness, neutrality, and progress. This is especially so if we see in addition that of all people anti-theists have no right to make any assumptions at all. They have left the theistic camp for the very reason that theism was altogether based upon the assumption or presupposition of an absolute self-conscious God. They would have none of such presuppositions, but rather began to investigate for themselves. Thus we must ask them to be true to their starting point, and we are not so ready to accept their conclusions once we see that the whole fabric of their thought is built upon one great assumption. We simply ask the anti-theist which assumption seems more reasonable to make for finite time-dependent man, the assumption of an absolute God or the assumption of an absolute man.

Which assumption is more reasonable? By their fruits ye shall know them. Theism was rejected, according to those who rejected it, because of great intellectual difficulties involved in its concepts. We would reject anti-theism in turn because it reduces all human experience and the whole of history to something meaningless. If there is no absolute God, himself the ultimate, eternal reality and as such the Creator of the space-time universe, there will not be any interpretation at all. There is then no unity to furnish any meaning to plurality. An ultimate plurality without an equally ultimate unity shatters all interpretation. The only basis of unity offered by anti-theism is that of a principle apart from personality, and a principle apart from personality can be no more than an abstract universal. Such an abstract universal has no comprehension because it has no existence of itself and therefore can furnish no basis of comprehension and interpretation for others. Anti-theism is based upon an assumption to which it has no right and which leads it to self-annihilation.

We have dwelt thus long upon Plato because his thought as a whole and his philosophy of education in particular is typical of all that we see and hear today. Modern philosophy has often tried the impossible in seeking to combine Christian theism with Platonic thought. Consequently we have with us many hybrid philosophies that easily deceive by their apparent similarity to theism. On the other hand the opposition to theism that was chiefly implicit in ancient times has become more explicit now. What were assumptions then are raised to first principles now.

Kant and the Modern Philosophy of Education

This increase in self-consciousness in general is particularly true with the Platonic assumption of the identity of nature of all thought, divine and human. Kant has raised this assumption to the position of the master principle of modern philosophy. Herein lay his Copernican revolution, although the really Copernican revolution was originally accomplished by Eve. According to Kant thought is *creatively constructive.* That is, *all* thought is creatively constructive, human as well as divine. That is real and is true which is in accordance with the laws of thought, and that is unreal and untrue which is not in accordance with the laws of thought. Such is Kant's contention. We see the same elevation of the abstract principle of thought to the highest possible metaphysical and epistemological status that we observed in Plato. We see now a more clearly avowed emphasis on man's equal originality with God. We see now a greater stress upon comprehensibility to man as a test of truth. Plato would, when pressed, make a desperate, can-do-no-harm appeal to revelation, but Kant has put away such childish things. He cannot accept anything from a Beyond. Nothing that finds no immediate response in and recognition by the laws of thought working in man's mind can be accepted. To do so would be to deny that human thought is creative. It is not only in the field of morality that Kant has declared man's independence. His independent morality is but the logical conclusion in one direction of the principle of the creativity of thought. This principle must work in every direction. Man, if creative, is altogether independent.

We do not expect that creation shall receive honorable mention from Kant. If human thought itself is essentially creative, how could it be created? Human thought, if created, would be primarily receptive and only secondarily creative. But for Kant human thought is primarily creative and therefore not created. Again, creation implies that God's thought alone is absolutely and originally creative. This original and exclusive creativity on the part of God is denied by Kant. God is creative, to be sure, but so is man. And, really, God's creativity is limited not only by man's equal creativity but also by law's independence. The God of theism is bowed out with thanks for past services, and another god is ushered in to do watchdog duty by the side of law.

It is this master principle of the creativity of human thought that holds in its grip with unquestioned predominance all modern philosophy in general and all modern philosophy of education in particular. It is against this master principle alone, as the heart of anti-theistic educational policy, that we fight. Fight not against anyone great or small, but against this king alone. Unmask this king! Take away his royal robe of boasted neutrality! Remove the plumes of principle and but an ugly assumption remains. Once this is done the theistic hosts need fear no longer.

But this exposure is not always easy. By skillful manipulation modern Idealism has taken Christian theistic phraseology into its system, though loading down each term with a content utterly foreign to its habits. Modern Idealism is like the elder son of Jesus' parable, professing faithfulness to the father but alienated from the father in his heart (Luke 15:29-32; see Matt. 21:30). Idealism speaks much of "creation," but by "creation" it means no more than logical dependence. And God is logically dependent upon man as well as man being logically dependent upon God. Hence one could speak of the creation of God about as well as of the creation of man. It is this that makes modern Idealism so dangerous to Christian theism. It has taught Modernism the art of putting new wine into old bottles without changing the labels. When Modernism speaks much of the beautiful Ideals to which Jesus devoted his life, it conceives of these Ideals as existing independently of God as well as independently of Jesus, and as such Modernism is not only anti-Christian, but anti-theistic as well. As long as Idealism and Modernism will not forsake the Kantian-Platonic assumption of the essential creativity of human thought, no theist can afford to raise the flag of peace.

Pragmatism and Modern Educational Theory

But we must bring the action of the Platonic-Kantian perspective more definitely up to date and into direct contact with educational policy today. You might be saying, "'Pragmatism' is in the air. John Dewey controls education today. It is evolution with which we struggle. Why not speak of them instead of spending so much time on Plato of pre-Christian times?" Yet I am persuaded that one can in no way deal satisfactorily with J. Dewey, with Pragmatism, and with evolution unless one has dealt with Plato and Kant. All that Pragmatism has done is to work out the Platonic-Kantian assumption in a particular and perhaps most logically consistent direction.

We have already seen that since anti-theistic rationalism had to deny creation, two and only two possible ways were open to it. The first was that of making all reality eternal; the second was that of making all reality temporal. Plato and modern Idealism have tried the former, and modern Idealism has been forced to begin to admit that it has run into a *cul de sac.* Time is too real, at least the illusion of time is too real, to be long denied. And since, by this hypothesis, God and man are subject to the same laws in the same way, it follows that if man can no longer breathe in the rarified air of the eternal and must come down to the valleys of time and space, God will have to come down with him. Pragmatism has therefore followed the second road as the only alternative to making all reality eternal; it has said that all reality is temporal. It has said, and said logically, that if Kant was right in saying that human thought is essentially creative, and man is a temporally conditioned being, then all reality is on the move. Orthodox Idealism has tried to exorcise this Galileo of Pragmatism, but under his breath he said, "It does move, nevertheless." Nothing could stop the force of logic. If Eve was right Plato was right; if Plato was right Kant was right; and if Kant was right John Dewey is right; and if John Dewey is right the anti-Christian, anti-theistic system of education is right.

Strange to say, however, even Pragmatism has not altogether rejected theistic-Christian terminology. The "creation" idea in particular has not been discarded. Henri Bergson speaks of "creative evolution." He thinks that he has made genuine room for creation once he has opposed mechanism and materialism, just as Kant thought he had made genuine room for religion and God just because he opposed a particular outgrowth of Rationalism. But what can "creation" mean apart from God? For Bergson the Void is God. Bare possibility as a shoreless and bottomless ocean envelopes the little speck of reality under our feet. Similarly S. Alexander speaks of Space, Time, and Deity. Deity is for him an ideal that a space-time originated humanity has somehow cast out as an anchor to an invisible sky. God is created as well as man, and of the two man appears earlier upon the screen. Here is the climax of the Platonic-Kantian principle. God has completely made the rounds. Instead of the Creator of the universe, he is created by the universe. He is to be an Omega without an Alpha.

Can education or interpretation on this basis appeal to God for its ordinance, for a *raison d'être* ("reason for existence," *ed.*)? Very clearly not. Man will not implicate himself into God's interpretation. Such interpretation no longer exists. If there is to be any warrant, ordinance, or reason for man's educational policy, it must lie in man himself. It is the deification of man, the number of man (Rev. 13:18).

But just here comes the difficulty. We have already seen that by its fruits ye shall know anti-theism. A basic pluralism without an equally basic unity, we saw, reduced experience to a meaningless something. This reduction to the meaningless of all experience as inherent in the Platonic-Kantian principle becomes most apparent in the case of Pragmatism. An avowed original pluralism with man as charter member has now become pluralism in flux. Time is made an inherent ingredient of all reality, and by this means rationality as we see it in man is made to drift on the void. The bold demand for complete comprehension found this universe too narrow if God were back of it. It has made room by removing God, but it has made too much room for itself. Man would not implicate himself into God's interpretation, but the removal of God's interpretation has also effected the removal of all interpretation. There is no longer a coherent universe into which man can implicate himself. The Platonic-Kantian principle has elevated law above God, above personality; but law is turned into license when thus elevated. Not one bit of reality can be said to be related to another bit; judgment, reason itself, is destroyed. There is no rationality in anything. Pragmatism is the younger son, the prodigal, realizing that his substance is being devoured, but the more loudly proclaiming the wisdom of his leaving the father's house.

When the Pragmatism, evolution, and neutralism largely in control of modern educational theory are thus seen to rest their whole program upon one assumption which leads to the destruction of every bit of reason for education itself, we ourselves take new courage. Whatever the intellectual difficulties involved in our view, we are not ready to accept the only substitute that is offered us. Is it poor advertising ethics to "run down" our competitor's product in order to sell our own? Nay, our business is not commercial. The analogy does not hold. We employ the ethics of Solomon when he pictured the consequences for those who loved the "strange woman," who appeared so fair and offered allurement—the emptiness of which was hard for healthful youth to see.

Only in passing would we call attention to the fact that our survey, however rapid, claims to be exhaustive. There is and can be no educational policy and practice not based upon the Platonic-Kantian rationalism except that of Christian theistic education. Recently there have been philosophers of education who reject Pragmatism and even reject Idealism to some extent. They want to be called theists. "Creation" is much in vogue with them. They speak of the will of God as the source of this world. They maintain the necessity of the transcendence of God. The reference is to A. S. Pringle-Pattison, C. C. J. Webb, H. Rashdall, J. Lindsay, and E. Hocking as philosophers, and K. Barth and E. Brunner as theologians. We most surely rejoice in their reaction against the immanentism of modern Idealism; but as long as avowedly or implicitly they still build upon the Platonic-Kantian principle of the creativity of human thought, we cannot accept their overtures of peace. A theism they may proclaim, but a theism that is at bottom hostile to the theism we desire.

Now, if the analysis we have sought to give of anti-theistic educational philosophy is true and exhaustive, it follows that our defense against or attack upon any particular educational policy should always keep this central principle in mind. The most important thing is not what particular form an anti-theistic educational philosophy assumes, but the important thing is and remains that it is anti-theistic. Pragmatism may be the most popular opponent of our educational policy today. Pragmatism may be the most outspokenly hostile to our views. It is natural that we should fight Pragmatism most. But let us beware lest fighting Pragmatism we make subtle entangling alliance with any idealistic or would-be theistic philosophy that may chance to have a minor quarrel with Pragmatism, too. Their quarrels are, after all, family quarrels; and since we fight against the family as such, we must take good care lest we harbor scorpions in our bosom. To play off the Assyrian against the Egyptian, or the Egyptian against the Assyrian, may be wise and legitimate; but an entangling alliance with either is everlastingly forbidden for a covenant people.

III. The Theistic-Christian Philosophy of Education[1]

We have said that Idealism was as the elder son and Pragmatism as the younger son of the parable when he refused to return though he already knew something of his folly. Now, to carry forth the analogy, we may call theism in general and our theistic-Christian philosophy of education in particular, the prodigal returned to the father's house because drawn by the father's love. In hot-headed haste we had denied creation and therewith our dependence upon the father's interpretation. In "riotous living" we had spent our substance, unwilling to admit that the land in which we dwelt was still the father's land. We had made the antithesis to God so great and final that no natural pendulum swing could, Hegelian-like, bring us to synthesis with God again. Only God himself could effect a synthesis between ourselves and him. Hence we do not wonder that others build upon and will not forsake an altogether unreasonable assumption. We do not expect men to be reasonable unless God has once more made them so. But this does not vitiate the usefulness of reasoning with unreasonable men. Such reasoning strengthens our faith, and (who knows?) may be used by the Spirit to make men reasonable.

It is thus that we return to the once discarded doctrine of creation. We do not accept it now because we no longer see or have solved all intellectual difficulties involved in it. But we have learned of the unreasonableness of the Platonic-Kantian assumption. We have learned that comprehension is no reasonable demand for man to make. We have now found that to seek for interpretation by ourselves apart from God leads to a fiasco, to self-stultification, and complete destruction. We now realize that we need a God who is himself and alone complete self-conscious rationality. If there is to be reason in anything under the sun, God must be absolute. He alone must be eternal since no eternity of ours could furnish comprehensive rationality. If we are made eternal with him, the case is hopeless because God is then reduced to one of us; if he is temporal with us, the case is, if possible, more hopeless still because then we have willfully cast all hope of coherence in experience overboard.

St. Augustine has already taught us this. His thought is at bottom the polar opposite of Plato's. For Plato the Ideas or laws are next to or higher than God; for Augustine the ideas or laws are expressive of God's nature. No more radical difference is conceivable. For Plato God wants the good because it is good in itself; for Augustine the good is good because God wants it and God wants it because it is expressive of his nature. For Augustine God's interpretation is prior even to the existence of the spatio-temporal universe. The universe is made according to God's plan. Would one interpret reality, would one interpret anything, one must find in it the plan of God. Once this plan is found, truth is found. Whether this truth be fully comprehensible to man or not, it is the truth nevertheless.

For St. Augustine human thought is primarily receptive and thereupon reconstructive. Man as a finite rational personality must live by revelation alone. His thought is not passive or inactive. In fact, true and fruitful activity exists only where true receptivity is found. No one but the theist finds sufficient friction to make advance in the slippery highways of interpretation. He alone does not jump from one ice lump to another in the midst of a torrential stream. He alone does not try to breathe in a vacuum. God must be external and man must be temporal, or there is no interpretation at all. And since only the notion of temporal creation provides for this distinction between God and man, it will now be clear that only the creation of man by God gives divine ordinance for education. Ours is a theistic system of education. If our policy of education is reasonable, is necessary, is the only reasonable system of education, it is because theism is reasonable, is necessary, is the only reasonable philosophy for man. Our system of education is as strong as theism is; therefore be not afraid but of good courage.

* * *

We have thus far purposely spoken of theistic instead of Christian education in order to call particular attention to the fact that those who reject our educational philosophy reject no "oddity" but reason itself. We have in this way already indicated that Christian education and theistic education are identical. It would seem to be useful to emphasize this fact. Sometimes we are tempted to doubt the value of our efforts, especially if we live in a community where the Bible is still read in the public schools and we are asked, nevertheless, to give freely of our hard-earned dollars for Christian education. When we face this temptation, the most helpful thing would seem to be to realize that, whatever the details may be, the whole of so-called neutral education is based upon the Platonic-Kantian principle of the independence of human thought and as such is diametrically opposed not only to Christianity but also to God. When this is clearly perceived, Christian education means to us more than a soteriological lifeboat, an institute of conversion. Christian education then becomes the *sine qua non* of human life itself; a true humanism and a genuinely human culture presupposes a temporal creation. Thus, the education not only of the Christian, but of the human being, of man as created, is a divinely ordained necessity.

The Theistic Foundation of Christian Education

What now remains to be done is to relate more definitely the superstructure of Christian or Reformed education to the theistic foundation we have sought to lay. Or rather, since theistic education has been identified with Christian education instead of made the foundation of Christian education, we must speak of our reasons for this identification. These reasons would not seem to be so immediately available. We ordinarily tend to think of theism as a philosophy only incidentally related to the Scriptures. And we are very shy lest our seeing a theistic foundation for Christianity and our making a good deal of a theistic defense of Christian education should weaken our firm belief in the testimony of the Spirit as the only real source of faith in Christianity. Yet I am firmly convinced that we must "hold to the one and not leave the other undone" (Matt. 23:23). A theistic defense of Christian education is not unnecessary because of, nor does it in the least affect our belief in, the all-determinative work of the Holy Spirit.

In the first place Christianity is a restorative religion. Christianity is theism restored and brought to its own. Christ came to bring man and his cosmos back to the God of creation. Those that accept salvation become true theists once more. They and they only are theists inasmuch as those that are not for the Christ are against him. The line of separation between theist and non-theist is just as clear as the line of separation between Christian and non-Christian because the one line carves more deeply the other line. Of course there are thousands that resent this way of putting things. Modernism wants to be called Christian. We can only answer that it is not only anti-Christian but anti-theistic as well. At least the Christianity and the theism it professes to hold are just as deadly hostile to the Christianity and the theism we profess to hold as could conceivably be. What then is there in the name?

As Christians we believe in the absoluteness of Christ. He said of himself, "I am the Way, the Truth and the Life" (John 14:6). That is, from him proceeds the Truth. Because of God, he does not testify to an independently existing principle of truth, but posits truth itself. This would be impossible unless Christ, as well as God the Father, were absolute eternally self-sufficient personality. The alternative is once more clear and exhaustive. If you would accept the Christ as he wants to be accepted, you must accept his identity with God not only but his identity with an absolute, comprehensively self-interpretative God. I cannot in any genuine sense be a Christian unless I believe in a God who alone interprets to me.

Accordingly Christ said that we must make his words the standard of belief and life. So Paul also says that every thought must be brought captive to the obedience of Christ. Obedience is not simply a response of subjection demanded by a conception of God as arbitrary ruler supposedly found in the Old Testament. Obedience to Christ is simply the receptively reconstructive attitude of the human being once more. It is this that Christ came to restore. Whether this receptivity reveals itself in the direction of matters pertaining immediately to salvation or not makes no difference. Christian or theistic culture, as well as immediate salvation, is controlled by the same receptivity principle of thought. Those that have not this receptivity have no salvation, but neither have they human culture.

What then becomes of all attempts to harmonize evolutionistic philosophy with Christianity? We speak now of evolutionistic philosophy as based upon the Platonic-Kantian principle of the open universe. Such philosophy, in all its forms, materialistic or vitalistic, Spencerian or Bergsonian, denies creation. And this is no detail. If creation be denied, the restorative character of Christianity is denied. How could Christ restore to man the receptively reconstructive attitude of mind if, never having been created by God, man never had such an attitude? Or, how could Christ restore anything if, because there is no creation, man could not be restored to anyone? Or again, how could Christ restore when, because there is no creation, he himself is but a prodigy with no possible significance for any human being? It is as impossible to deny Christianity and preserve theism as it is impossible to deny theism and preserve Christianity. It is as impossible to oppose Christian education and be genuinely interested in human culture as it is to deny human culture and be interested in Christian education; a foundation without a roof affords no shelter, and a roof without a foundation affords no room.

Circular Reasoning and the Absolute Authority of Scripture

But the charge will finally be made that I accept all this because the Bible tells me. The Bible tells me that its God and its Christ are absolute and the sole source of interpretation. The Bible tells me that obedience is a covenant obligation because it is an implication of creation. But whence my belief in the Bible? If my reply is that an absolute God and an absolute Christ need an absolutely authoritative Bible in a sinful world, the logic is granted. Such is surely the case. If sin is what Scripture says it is, a denial of man's receptivity of heart and mind, if God is what Scripture says he is, an absolute God, and if Christ is what Scripture says he is, the restorer of man to God, then only an infallibly inspired Scripture can help make men theists again. But how do I know that what the Bible says is true? If I say that it accords with my experience, I do not escape the charge of circle reasoning, because admittedly my experience has been molded under the influence of the Scriptures. If I say that Scripture accords with a theism that I find more satisfactory than any other philosophy, I again do not escape the charge of circle reasoning because I have just stated that my theism, too, comes from the Scriptures. How then shall I escape the charge of circle reasoning when men ridicule me because as an educator I assume the authority of Scripture?[2]

The answer is that I shall in no wise seek to escape it but boldly affirm it as the only alternative to self-destruction. What I shall do is first show clearly on the one hand that belief in an absolute God, creation, and man's original receptivity of thought—that is, theism—is indissolubly connected with and restored by Christ and Scripture, that is, by Christianity; and on the other hand that belief in a finite God, an uncreated universe, and the essential creativity of human thought—that is, antitheism—is indissolubly connected with a denial of Christ's divinity and the authority of Scripture, that is, with anti-Christianity. Then, when I have done this, I gladly admit and avow that I am a theist and a Christian because the Holy Spirit has made me so, but I equally maintain that all men should be theists and Christians because only theism and Christianity can offer meaning to experience at all. Circular reasoning is the most reasonable form of reasoning for a finite personality. No other form of reasoning is possible.

When as Christian educators we have thus seen things as a whole and have seen them through, we make no mean apologies for teaching children with authority. Nor do we fear that biblical criticism and evolutionism may tomorrow make our position untenable. Nor yet do we wildly dash for a would-be up-to-dateness in methods of pedagogy and psychology. What shall we teach and how can we teach at all if not with the authority of God and Christ? How shall the facts of Scripture or nature ever disprove the existence of an absolute God, if only an absolute God could make such facts? Or how can modern psychology tell us of the needs of the human being, unless it ask of Christ and God what these needs may be? A certain independence of spirit we need in our Christian education. Not, of course, the independence of those who ridicule us. That is the independence of pride. And such independence of spirit is the denial of our whole position. But yet, an independence we need. An independence we need that has cast out crouching fear. We are right, not by our wisdom but through God. And because we are right through the work of the Spirit, it behooves us to be humbly bold. If God is for us, who can be against us?

A Consistently Christian Philosophy of Education

Would that all Christians saw the logic of their Christianity! They would not then seek salvation for eternity alone by haphazard, nervous methods of revivalism, of individualistic preaching and teaching, and thus fail in large measure to accomplish what they set out to do. In covenant education we seek not to extract the human being from his natural milieu as a creature of God, but rather to restore the creature with his milieu to God. Incomparably the wiser is this method since it transplants the plant with, instead of without, its soil. Incomparably the more consistent is this method because Christianity itself claims to be restorative and supplementative of theism. Obedience is the subjective principle of the covenant. Obedience is also the subjective principle of a creature. A Christian is a true human being once more.

Once we have seen this whole and have seen it through, the argument that the Sunday school, the catechism, and the church are sufficient for our educational purposes loses all its plausibility and charm. Such an argument denies that Christianity is a true theism. Such an argument denies the restorative character of Christianity. Such an argument would seek to patch Christianity upon an anti-theistic foundation and thus eventually destroy Christianity itself. There is an element of anti-theism in every form of inconsistent Christianity. Only a Reformed philosophy of education is a consistently Christian philosophy of education, and it alone is free from self-destructive germs. Only it should be added that we are far from boasting that we are actually to the full extent Reformed in all our educational efforts; we are striving for the ideal.

If we would be polemically self-conscious as well as apologetically self-conscious—and the one is scarcely possible without the other—we must briefly note how in distinction from Roman Catholicism and Lutheranism the Reformed principle of education is alone consistently Christian and theistic.

It is not necessary to point out in detail the anti-theistic elements in Roman Catholic theology and philosophy. We would note something of them insofar as they have bearing upon education. We sometimes say that Rome is following a consistent policy of authority in education. Yet Rome has always tried in vain to harmonize something of the Platonic-Kantian principle of the creativity of human thought with the receptivity theory of Christianity. Hence its strange coordination of Scripture and tradition. Hence its strange doctrine of gradation of priest above "layman" in general, and its strangest possible doctrine of papal infallibility in particular. Hence also the necessity of enforcing authority by external means. Rome's principle is weak because it is inconsistent. Rome's apparent strength is due to the element of truth in her principle and, in addition to this, due to extraneous circumstances. Rome cannot make a consistent stand against unbelief today nor in the future; it maintains itself by compromise. It is well that we emphasize the fact that we have much in common with Rome, but never should we forget that it is up to those that are Reformed to furnish the only consistent and therefore the only finally effective apologetic against unbelief.

Then as to Lutheranism, it may with joy be said that it harbors less of anti-theism in its bosom than does Roman Catholicism. Yet even Lutheranism has its pantheistic elements. Lutheranism has not clearly grasped the significance of the creation idea. It has not always firmly maintained that God is eternal and man is temporal. By ascribing omnipresence to the human nature of Christ, Lutheranism toned down the distinction between the temporal and the eternal. And the reason for this was that there is even in Lutheranism a remnant of Platonic rationalism. Man is given some independent power of interpretation. Principle is not always clearly maintained to be subordinate to the absolute personality of God. Man's thoughts need not in every respect be led captive to the obedience of Christ. The meaning of obedience is not fully understood; the whole covenant idea is practically ignored. Consequently culture is but loosely related to Christianity. What then can the Lutheran system of education accomplish? Very much indeed, but not enough. Lutheran educational policy must eventually tolerate an unbiblical rift between Christianity and theism; the natural will not be sanctified by the supernatural. Lutheran educational philosophy cannot meet the enemy of Christianity and theism at every sector of the front.

Conclusion

Our conclusion can be none other than that in the Reformed philosophy of education we have Christian education come to its own, and in the Christian philosophy of education we have theistic education come to its own. The numerous ordinances for divine education as we find them in the Scriptures are expressions of one grand covenant principle, and this grand covenant principle rests upon the idea of temporal creation as its presupposition and, back of the created universe, upon an absolute God. Not one of these ideas can one retain unless he retains them all. Together they stand or together they fall. This we would have our enemies see. How seldom do we find an enemy challenging our system of ideas or attacking our philosophy of education in its central principle of the essential receptivity of the human mind! Ready we are to avow this principle unabashed. As Luther stood in the Diet of Worms, surrounded by an overwhelmingly powerful enemy, saying that he could not possibly retract his faith, so we stand before the bar of the educational philosophy of the day. That philosophy must condemn us. That philosophy assumes, and then sets out to prove, that the temporal-spatial universe has *not* been created by an absolute God; yet it is only the presupposition of this Creator which makes reasoning and proof possible. Hence we are not afraid or ashamed. Mighty is the truth and it will conquer at last.

4

COVENANT: THE COVENANT OF GRACE AND ITS SIGNIFICANCE FOR CHRISTIAN EDUCATION

LOUIS BERKHOF

Advocates of Christian education have always maintained that the Christian school is an outgrowth of the covenant idea and is absolutely necessary in order to enable the child to appreciate his covenant privileges and to understand the solemn significance of his baptism in the name of the triune God. They are convinced that the Christian school, as well as infant baptism, finds its main support in the doctrine of the covenant; and they are therefore unalterably opposed to the tendency of some to slight this doctrine and to relegate it to the background.

In the American ecclesiastical world the doctrine of the covenant is almost entirely unknown. You can take up one work on systematic theology after another without finding a single chapter devoted to it. Such works as those of the Hodges, Thornwell, and Dabney form exceptions to the rule.[1] Moreover, it is quite evident that in most of the churches of our land, even in those who theoretically subscribe to the doctrine of the covenant, this doctrine has no grasp on the life and the conscience of the people in general, and fails utterly to have a determining influence on the education of their children.

In the present controversy between the Modernists and the Fundamentalists the hearts of all serious-minded Christians naturally go out to the latter, because they take their stand on the infallible Word of God. Unfortunately, however, they are nearly all Premillennialists, who drive a wedge between the Old and the New Testaments, claim that the covenant made with Abraham and sealed by circumcision includes only the natural descendants of the patriarch, and therefore deny that we and our children have any part in it and that this is sealed to us by baptism. Experience has already taught us that those who come under the spell of

Premillennialism finally lose their covenant conception and turn to the position of the Baptists.

Occasionally some well-meaning persons in our circles express the fear that we speak too much about the covenant and are in danger of making people averse to it. Now there may have been a time when this fear was warranted, but in our opinion it is quite unnecessary at present. There is more point to the oft-repeated complaint that in our day the doctrine of the covenant is not stressed as it ought to be. And even if the fear expressed were perfectly justified, that would be no reason that we should refrain from discussing this subject. It is a striking fact that, while the advocates of Christian education always insisted on the close relation between the covenant idea and the Christian school, I have not been able to lay my hand on a single book or pamphlet, either in the Holland or in the English language, devoted to a discussion of the subject in question.

The fact is that in our struggle for Christian schools the doctrine of the covenant was always the great presupposition. The relation in which the covenant idea stands to the Christian school may have been discussed time and again in sermons and lectures that did not appear in print. On the printed page we find an occasional reference to the fact that the children of Christian parents should be religiously educated in view of the fact that they are covenant children, and that, when they were brought to baptism, their parents promised to provide such an education for them. But nowhere do we find this idea worked out. Hence it can hardly be regarded as superfluous that a paper be devoted to the relation of the covenant idea and the Christian education which we desire for our children. Even so the presentation of it can hardly be commensurate with its great importance.

I. The Covenant of Grace

The Idea of Covenant

For a proper understanding of the covenant of grace it is quite essential that we have some conception of the covenant idea in general. It can hardly escape the attention of Bible students that, while the essential elements of the covenant of grace are already present in the *Protevangelium,*[2] its formal establishment is introduced comparatively late in the history of revelation. It was nearly twenty centuries after the creation of the world that God formally entered into covenant relationship with Abraham and his seed. And there was a perfectly good reason for this delay in the general method of divine relation, in which the natural precedes the spiritual, and spiritual realities are presented in forms derived from the natural world. Under the providence of God the various forms of life, of the interactions of the social groups, and of the associations among men, were first brought to development in the natural life of men, and were then used by God as the vehicles of his special revelation.

Thus people had to grow accustomed to the idea of covenant agreements first, before God could utilize such an idea in the revelation of the eternal verities of the covenant of grace. And then he employed it, first of all, in the revelation of the so-called covenant of nature with Noah, and only after that in revealing the covenant of grace with believers and their seed.

The necessity of entering into covenant agreements was felt first of all by individuals and tribes that were brought into close relation with each other and had no authority above them to secure their mutual rights and privileges. They sought the coveted security by entering into a voluntary agreement in which the mutual obligations and rights of both parties were clearly set forth and fully secured. A covenant so made, and often ratified by drinking sacrificial blood, eating a sacrificial meal, or eating salt together, was held to be most sacred and binding. It was not, as a rule, an expression of that self-seeking spirit that is so characteristic of modern international covenants or agreements, but generally resulted from a genuine desire for a closer union, more intimate relationship, lasting friendship, and mutual devotion.

But though the covenant idea first found expression in the natural life of man and was only after that embodied in the divine revelation, it should not be thought that the human covenants were the original and real covenants, and that the covenant of God with believers and their seed is only a copy of these, or that this idea is merely a figure used to express the close relation between God and his people. If we turn this right around, we are nearer to the truth. God's covenant is the divine original, and all covenants among men are but faint reflections of it; it is not a mere figure of speech but a blessed reality rich in promises and full of heavenly comfort.

If we reflect for a moment on the covenants that were so frequently established among men, especially in the early patriarchal times, we cannot but notice that they are marked by certain definite characteristics. There are always two parties in such a covenant (in fact, a covenant of one party would be a contradiction in terms), and these parties are of such a kind that they can meet on a footing of equality. There are also two parts in every covenant; each party solemnly pledges himself to the performance of certain duties and in turn is assured of the fulfillment of certain promises. And the guarantee that the covenant requirements will be met and that the covenant promises will be fulfilled does not lie in any superior power that can and will force the parties to meet their mutual obligations, if need be, but only in the sacred character of the agreement and in the honor and faithfulness of the covenanting parties.[3]

The Covenant of Grace

Now let us take a closer view of the covenant of grace. We do not intend—and in fact, it would be quite impossible—to discuss this in all its details, but will only stress the points that need elucidation in an intelligent discussion of this subject. We generally speak of the covenant of grace as being that gracious compact or agreement between the offended God and the offending sinner, in which God promises salvation through faith in Christ and the sinner accepts this believingly. It may be well to use an illustration that will serve to bring out just what the covenant of grace involves, before we stress some of the more important particulars of the covenant relation. We should bear in mind, however, that the illustration conveys to us only an imperfect approximation of the truth.

Let us imagine a rich and beneficent slave-holder with a thousand slaves, who are in duty bound to labor faithfully for their master, without any claim to reward, it is true, but with the assurance that, after a period of faithful labor, they will obtain their freedom. After a period of scrupulous attention to duty the slaves gradually grow restive under the yoke, begin plotting against their master, vent their dissatisfaction in murmurings and grumbling and muttered curses, which like the distant thunder announce the coming storm, and finally break into an open revolt in which they seek to shake off their fetters and to overthrow once for all the regime of their landlord. But the latter is well disposed toward his mutinous bond-servants and is anxious to raise them to a higher level. So he himself opens the way to a full and free pardon, though it involves a great deal of self-sacrifice, and resorts to all possible means to insure their future obedience. He even condescends to come down to their level and to deal with them as on a footing of equality. He makes a compact with them, in which he promises to pardon their insurrection, to adopt them and their children into his own family with the full rights and privileges of children, and to make them and their descendants heirs of his extensive possessions; and they, in turn, accept his pardon on the stipulated conditions, vow obedience to him as their lord, and pledge themselves to his service. Naturally they, as bond-servants, were in duty bound to accept whatever arrangement their master might make, and after the compact was closed they were doubly obliged to honor its provisions. Moreover, it was in their interest that they should live up to the terms of the agreement, since it opened up the brightest prospects for them and their children, and brought to them what they could in no way hope to merit by their labors—a congenial home, the precious gift of liberty, untold riches, the pleasure of life, and a choice society in which to move.

Now if we reflect on this covenant arrangement which may, at least in a measure, serve to illustrate the agreement between God and the sinner in the covenant of grace, we shall notice that, while it certainly has all the essential characteristics of a covenant, it is yet marked by certain peculiarities. There are in this, as in every other covenant, two parties; but the parties are not of such a nature that they can meet on a footing of equality. This is something unusual. We do not ordinarily find a slave-holder making a covenant with his slaves. In his estimation they have no rights that would entitle them to such consideration. He simply issues his commands, and expects them to obey.

Thus our attention is directed at once to a very important feature of the covenant of grace. The distance between God and man is infinitely greater than that between a landlord and his slave, for the latter does not transcend the measure of the purely human. However different their social standing may be, the master and the bond-servants are all men and in that respect equals, and even the latter have certain rights which the former may not disregard. But God is far greater than man; he gives no account of his doings; he is not under obligation to any of his creatures. To the sorely afflicted Job, crushed and perplexed, who had shown an inclination to question the doings of the Almighty, he says: "Who then is he that can stand before me? Who hath first given unto me, that I should repay him? Whatsoever is under the whole heaven is mine" (Job 41:10, 11). Man has absolutely no rights in relation to God. God has but to command, and man is in duty bound to obey. And not only that, but sinful man has actually forfeited his life, and forfeited whatever rights he might have had in virtue of an original divine grant.

In the covenant of grace, therefore, we find two very unequal parties: the infinite God, the Creator of the universe, "glorious in holiness, fearful in praises, doing wonders" (Exod. 15:11), and finite man, a transient creature of the dust, sinful and polluted. The one is the rich possessor of all things, man included, and the other merely a steward of treasures entrusted to his care; the one has rightful claims on the life, the possessions, the time, and the service of his creatures, and is under no obligation to them, and the other is in duty bound to render all to God and yet obtains no claim to any reward; the one can offer riches and honor and joys beyond compare, and the other can offer nothing, not even the bankrupt life which he sometimes calls his own.

In view of this fact it is no wonder that some theologians do not regard what we usually call "the covenant of grace" as a covenant at all, but prefer to speak of it simply as a divine arrangement, a gracious disposition, or a testament, thus stressing the one-sided character of the transaction. And undoubtedly, in its origin and in its effective operation, the covenant is one-sided. At the same time it is clearly represented as a covenant in Scripture, and being essentially a covenant, it is necessarily of the nature of an agreement between two parties. God condescended to come down to the level of man in the covenant of works, and promised to reward a temporary obedience with life eternal. Again, he condescended to come down to the level of *sinful* man in Christ, and now in the covenant of grace offers eternal life to all that accept Christ by faith. The gracious element that was present even in the first covenant is far more pronounced in the second. What condescending love in God to enter into covenant relationship with sinners in Christ! Well may we be grateful for the dignity thus bestowed upon us, sinful creatures.

In the illustration used I pointed out that it involved a great deal of self-sacrifice on the part of the landlord to enter into covenant relation with his bond-servants. The same thing applies where God enters into a covenant of grace with sinners. He could not simply come down to the level of willful transgressors and make a covenant with them without maintaining his justice and safeguarding his holiness. He could deal with sinners only in the person of someone who undertook it voluntarily to be their surety and who guaranteed that the demands of justice would be met both objectively and subjectively, i.e., that the inflexible justice of God would be satisfied by a sacrificial death, that the original demand of the law would be met by a life of obedience, and that those who would share in the blessings of forgiveness would also consecrate their lives to God. Now there is nothing peculiar in the fact that there should be a surety in the covenant of grace. This is a rather common occurrence in covenants. The moral or financial standing of one of the parties to a transaction may be of a rather dubious character, thus making a surety or guarantor quite essential. In our day great companies exist for the purpose of supplying the necessary bonds. But in the covenant of grace the striking thing is this, that the party known to be absolutely reliable himself supplies a surety for the bankrupt party with which he is dealing. God gives his only-begotten Son, and the Son voluntarily takes it upon himself to become a surety for lost and helpless sinners. Here too the gracious nature of the covenant shines forth.

> Wouldst thou learn the depth of sin,
> All its bitterness and pain?
> What it cost thy God to win
> Sinners to Himself again?
> Come, poor sinner, come with me;
> Visit sad Gethsemane.
> Wouldst thou know God's wondrous love?
> Seek it not beside the throne;
> List not angels' praise above,
> But come and hear the heavy groan
> By the Godhead heaved for thee,
> Sinner, in Gethsemane.

The Promise of the Covenant of Grace

The gracious nature of the covenant also appears very clearly from another point of view. In every covenant there are two elements, promises and requirements; and this also applies to the covenant of grace. These elements find expression in the oft-repeated words: "I will be their God; and they shall be my people." But though there are also requirements in the covenant of grace, the promises are very much in the foreground; in fact, all the requirements are also covered by divine promises. It was in the consciousness of that blessed fact that Augustine prayed: "Lord, give what Thou commandest, and then command what Thou wilt."

The promises of the covenant are exceedingly comprehensive. The basic promise is that of the forgiveness of sins. Sin raised a barrier between God and man which must first of all be removed. As long as it is not taken out of the way, the sinner lies under a sentence of condemnation; he has no approach to God, cannot ascend his holy hill, and cannot stand in his presence. Fellowship with God is entirely out of the question. But when sin is pardoned, the sentence of condemnation is lifted, the way to the tree of life is opened, and the sinner can again find rest at the bosom of his heavenly Father.

Inseparably connected with the pardoning grace of God is the grace of adoption. God adopts sinners into his own family. This implies, of course, that they are not children of God by nature. If they were, this adoption would be entirely out of the question. Parents can adopt a child, but they cannot adopt their own children. This is the blessing of which John speaks when he says, "But as many as received him, to them gave He the right to become children of God, even to them that believe on His name" (John 1:12). It is the blessing in which Paul rejoices, "For ye received not the spirit of bondage again unto fear; but ye received the spirit of adoption, whereby we cry, Abba, Father" (Rom. 8:15).

With the blessing of adoption another blessing goes hand in hand. Sinners are made children of God, not merely in a legal sense by means of adoption, but also in a spiritual sense of regeneration and sanctification. God does much more than man can ever hope to do when he takes a child into his family. Parents can adopt a child, but cannot transform it. They cannot change the inner nature of the child, cannot impart to it their characteristic traits, and cannot make it resemble them. God is not only abundantly able to accomplish this, but actually brings it to pass. He sends forth the Spirit of his Son into the hearts of sinners, crying, "Abba, Father." He restores in them the image of God, renews their lives, and creates within them a new spirit of obedience, so that as true children they become desirous and even anxious to do the Father's will.

But there is still more. Sonship includes heirship with all its privileges. Unworthy sinners, who have forfeited the least of the blessings of God, fall heir to ethical and spiritual perfections, to the most intimate and loving communion with God in Christ Jesus, and to the eternal glories of their heavenly King. They receive an inheritance incorruptible and undefiled and that fadeth not away in the city of the living God, the heavenly Jerusalem, where they as the church of the firstborn in the company of innumerable hosts of angels will walk in the light of the Lamb and will enjoy perfect peace and happiness in endless life.

We have given only the barest indications of what is included in the promises of the covenant. There are promises for the present and for the future, promises for days of prosperity and for seasons of adversity, promises for the living and for the dying. There are promises of renewed strength for those whose strength seems to fail, promises of courage for the faint-hearted and of rest for the weary. There are promises of guidance through life and of deliverance out of temptations, promises of the support of the everlasting arms and of good cheer for the afflicted and the discouraged, promises of security for storm-tossed souls, promises, too, of an everlasting home for weary pilgrims.

Oh, wonderful story of deathless love,
Each child is dear to that heart above!
He fights for me when I cannot fight;
He comforts me in the gloom of night;
He lifts the burden, for He is strong;
He stills the sigh and wakes the song;
The sorrows that bear me down, He shares,
And loves and pardons because He cares.

Let all who are sad take heart again,
We are not alone in our hours of pain;
Our Father looks from His throne above
To soothe and comfort us with His love.
He leaves us not when the storms are high;
And we have safety, for He is nigh.
Can that be trouble, which He doth share?
Oh, rest in peace, for the Lord will care!

And the promises—all the promises, as many promises as there are and that are yea and amen in Christ Jesus—are for us *and for our children.* That is the glad assurance we have in the covenant of grace. Hence Christian parents who take their baptismal vows seriously may always plead these promises for their offspring.

The Requirements of the Covenant of Grace

But now it is time to remind ourselves once more of the fact that there are two elements in the covenant, promises and requirements. This is all the more necessary because there are some really pious people who are inclined to deny that there are any requirements in the covenant of grace. They regard this denial necessary in order to avoid the errors of Pelagianism and of Arminianism. They are anxious to maintain the position that the work of salvation is a work of the grace of God from the beginning to the end, and that man contributes absolutely nothing to it. Hence they are averse to the idea that the covenant of grace is in any sense conditional. Let us consider this question for a moment. Is the covenant of grace conditional or is it not? This question cannot be answered by a simple negative or affirmative, but must be answered with careful discrimination.

If we consider the foundation of the covenant, we find it to be just as conditional as the covenant of works. Just as the covenant of works was conditioned on the obedience of Adam, so the covenant of grace is conditioned on the suffering and obedience, in short, on the merits of Jesus Christ. It is only on the basis of his atoning work that we can share in the blessings of the covenant of grace. But since all are agreed here, it is quite evident that this is not the exact point at issue. The real question is whether there is any condition with which we must comply, in order to enter the covenant and to obtain the covenant blessings and the covenant end for ourselves and for our children.

Now it is implied in the very idea of a covenant that there should be conditions; if there were none, there would be no covenant. Moreover, the Bible clearly teaches us that there are certain conditions. But the word *conditions* is not always used in the same sense, and it is possible to use it in a sense which does not apply in the covenant of grace. There is no condition attached to the covenant of grace which includes the idea of merit on the part of man. Because Christ has merited all the blessings of the covenant, the idea that man should merit anything is absolutely excluded. Moreover, there is no condition which man must fulfill in his own strength. He is constantly reminded of the fact that he needs strength from above in order that he may answer to the requirements of the covenant. Bearing these things in mind, however, we undoubtedly can speak of certain prerequisites for entering the covenant, for sharing the life of the covenant, and for obtaining the full covenant blessings.

People enter the covenant relationship either by birth from Christian parents, or, if they are not born within the pale of the church, by a profession of faith in Christ. They become conscious partakers of the covenant life only by a saving faith in Jesus Christ that is wrought in their hearts by the Holy Spirit, a faith by which they merit nothing but simply appropriate Christ as the fountain of all spiritual blessings. And they obtain the full possession and enjoyment of the covenant blessings and of the glorious covenant inheritance only by faith and sanctification, by separation from the world in consecration to God, and by a life of childlike and loving obedience. In the case of Christian parents this naturally involves the duty that they be diligent in training their children in the fear and admonition of the Lord, in order that these children, when they come to maturity, may willingly take upon themselves their covenant obligations and may, with their parents, enjoy the rich covenant blessings.

In this connection it is highly necessary to bear in mind that living in the covenant relationship is something more than living under the gospel, under the free offer of salvation. There is here something more than an offer, something more than a promise; there is an agreement. The covenant is an *established covenant*, a *covenant agreed to*, agreed to by parents *also for their children*. When they sought the seal of baptism for their offspring, they promised, as Joshua did in the days of old: "as for me *and my house*, we will serve Jehovah." This means that, for the children of the covenant, the covenant is not merely an offer which they can accept or reject, but an agreement which they entered; and that, if they do not live up to the terms of the agreement, they are covenant-breakers. Even as creatures of God they were already in duty bound to accept whatever arrangement he made for them. But in virtue of the agreement entered by their parents also in their behalf, they have an added responsibility. They are now doubly obliged to honor the covenant, to live into it, and to meet its requirements with grateful hearts.

It may be said that when Christian parents make such a promise they promise more than they can accomplish, for they cannot impart the new life to their children, cannot create within them the spirit of obedience. Now it is perfectly true that the parents cannot guarantee spiritual renewal; nor does God expect or require it of them. They make their promise entirely on the strength of the promises of God. If they promise to intercede for their children, to educate them in the fear of the Lord, and to set them an example of true Christian piety, they simply promise to utilize the means which God has ordained for the realization of the covenant life in their children; and they have the blessed assurance that God will enable them to meet these covenant requirements. And if they promise that they with their children will fear the Lord, they do it in trustful reliance on the never failing promises of God that he will work in those children and create within them a clean heart and a willing spirit.

Occasionally we meet with people who consider it reprehensible that parents make such a promise for their children. They claim that the parents have absolutely no right to enter into such an agreement for their offspring. The children should be allowed to choose for themselves when they come to maturity. But suppose that some beneficent capitalist offered poor parents untold riches, and offered to extend his munificence also to their children provided the parents would educate them into a right appreciation and a grateful acceptance of that wealth and the children would show themselves worthy of it by a good moral conduct—and suppose that the parents accepted the offer and entered the agreement for themselves and for their children, promising to do all that lay in their power to meet the conditions. Could that rightly be considered as an injustice to the children? And would it not be utter folly on the part of the children to break the agreement? Children of Christian parents have every reason to be thankful that, along with their parents, they stand in a blessed covenant relation.

II. The Covenantal Basis of Christian Education

Now the question arises, How does the covenant relationship furnish a basis for Christian education? Our form of baptism clearly implies that there is a close connection between the two.[4] Only three questions are put to the parents, and of these three one concerns itself entirely with the matter of Christian education. The first question seeks recognition of the fact that, though our children are born in sin and therefore subject to condemnation, they are nevertheless sanctified in Christ and as such entitled to baptism. The second requires a renewed confession of the parents that the doctrine contained in Scripture and taught in our church is the true and perfect doctrine of salvation. And the third exacts of them the promise that they will be faithful and diligent in teaching their children that glorious saving truth. The first is expressive of the title which the children of Christian parents have to baptism; the second, of the parents' right to seek baptism for their children; and the third, of the obligation that is involved in the privilege.

It is deserving of notice that the promise is a very comprehensive one. The parents publicly assume the responsibility of instructing their children in the "aforesaid doctrine"; and this is not merely the doctrine of the covenant, as some have asserted, but the doctrine contained in the Old and New Testament, the whole round of Christian truth with its broad sweep, touching every realm, every sphere, and every relation of Christian life. Thus we have a very clear indication of the spirit that ought to permeate the instruction of covenant children.

And now we repeat the question: In what way does the covenant relation involve the duty to give the children of the covenant a truly Christian education? There are especially three lines of thought that suggest themselves here. Let us consider these for a few moments.

Adoption and the Honor of God

In the *first* place this necessity is involved in the fact that the children of Christian parents are, with their parents, adopted into the family of God. Think for a moment of the illustration that was used at the beginning of our discussion. The generous landlord adopted his bond-servants and their children into his family. But in doing this he at once encountered the problem of their education. The privilege which he bestowed upon them made it incumbent on them to live on a higher cultural level, to move about in refined company from day to day, and to reflect their high station in life in their habits and customs and general manner of living. All of these things would be quite impossible for them unless they were educated and trained for that new life of culture and refinement. It would be but natural, therefore, that the landlord should make provision for the necessary education of his bond-servants and should make arrangements which would insure a corresponding education for their children. He naturally could not permit them to degrade his name; rather, he would want them to be an honor to it.

Now, the children of the covenant are adopted into a family that is infinitely higher than the family of any man of rank or nobility. They are adopted into the family of the covenant God himself. Even while on earth they are privileged to join the company of the redeemed, the saints of God. They take their place in the church of Jesus Christ, which is the heavenly Jerusalem. Moreover, they are destined to live and move about eternally in the company of just men made perfect, of the innumerable hosts of the angels of God, and of Jesus Christ, the King all-glorious. Perfect life in the most intimate communion with the triune God is their grand destiny; heaven with all its glories is their eternal home. Can we at all doubt whether this calls for Christian education? Can we really suggest in all seriousness that in a world such as we are living in Christian education in the home, in the church, and in the Sunday school is quite adequate? Ought we not rather to ask, Is the best religious education we can give our children, no matter how comprehensive and how thorough, really commensurate with the high dignity to which our children are called? Should we not bend all our efforts to make it richer and fuller, and to bring it more into harmony with their high calling and their exalted duties? Would we want our children to be a dishonor to the household of God? Let us ever be mindful of the fact that the King's children must have a royal education.

The Promises of the Covenant

The necessity of Christian education follows, in the *second* place, also from the fact that the children of Christian parents fall heir to the covenant promises. The master making a covenant with his slaves pardoned their insurrection, endowed them with material riches, and made them co-heirs with his own children. This is the very thing that God does in the covenant of grace. Now suppose that our children had been robbing some wealthy landowner and were caught in the act, and that this landowner did not prosecute them, but instead heaped coals of fire upon their heads by making them the heirs of untold riches. Would not this at once suggest a new duty to us, the duty to impress upon our children their utter unworthiness and the munificence of him whom they sought to deprive of his possessions, and to make them fully conscious of the immense wealth so magnanimously bestowed upon them and of the responsibility which it involved? It is quite evident that this would appear desirable for more than one reason. We would naturally feel it incumbent on us to engender in our children a spirit of true gratitude, to promote their happiness by helping them to obtain a proper realization of their great riches, and teach them the right use of their sudden wealth.

Children of Christian parents, in spite of their unworthiness, fall heir to the blessed promises of the covenant, and these promises cover the whole range of life, natural and spiritual, temporal and eternal, and as such guarantee them all the riches of grace and glory that are in Christ Jesus. These bounties naturally call for gratitude. God expects his covenant children to praise him with thankful hearts. The unthankful are classed with the notoriously wicked (II Tim. 3:2). After Moses had reminded the children of Israel of their covenant privileges and had pointed to the blessing which they were about to receive in Palestine, he said unto them, "And thou shalt eat and be full, and thou shalt bless Jehovah thy God for the good land which He hath given thee" (Deut. 8:10). Our children too must bring their thank-offerings to the Lord. But how can they be adequately thankful unless they are taught to see how much they have received? They should be brought to a realization of the fact that never ending thanks are due and that even the best they can bring to the Lord is but an inadequate expression of the gratefulness they owe their covenant God. If the question of the poet finds an echo in their heart—

What shall I render to the Lord
For all His benefits to me?
How shall my soul by grace restored
Give worthy thanks, O Lord, to Thee?

—then Christian education must help them to find an appropriate answer.

It may be shown also from another angle that the rich promises of the covenant naturally call for Christian education. If the promises of God, which constitute the true riches of all the children of God, are to promote the real happiness and blessedness of their recipients, these must learn to understand the wide bearing of these promises and to know what treasures they include. Let us remember that, subjectively, we are no richer than our comprehension of what we possess, and that it is the true appreciation of our wealth which determines the measure of enjoyment derived from it. New Testament believers are more blessed than those of the Old Testament because they have a clearer conception of their covenanted riches. Jesus said to his disciples, "Blessed are your eyes, for they see; and your ears, for they hear. For verily I say unto you, that many prophets and righteous men desired to see the things which ye see, and saw them not; and to hear the things which ye hear, and heard them not" (Matt. 13:16, 17). Many children of God are even today living in spiritual poverty, though they are rich in Christ and heirs of the world, because they have not been taught to see the greatness and splendor of their spiritual heritage. If we do not want our children to live as paupers in spiritual penury and want while untold riches of grace and mercy are at their disposal, we must employ all the means at our command to unfold before their very eyes the treasures of divine grace of which they are heirs in Christ Jesus.

Once again, the promises of the covenant necessitate Christian education, because they inevitably impose upon our children a heavy responsibility. If all other things are equal, the affluent man has a far greater responsibility than the man of small means. He may not squander his wealth; on the contrary, he must invest it to the best advantage. And if he is not a born financier, he will need careful training for the proper administration of his wealth. Inherited riches often become a curse for the recipient because he has not been trained in the proper administration and use of money. Through lack of training the whole inheritance is sometimes lost. And may we not say of our children, to whom God entrusts great wealth in his covenant promises, that they are not all born stewards in the household of God? Yet stewards they must be, for God has enriched them with spiritual treasures in order that they should administer this wealth for the honor of his name and for the extension of his kingdom. Are we warranted in assuming that they will naturally be faithful to their trust and will make the best possible use of their God-given possessions? Are there no reasons to fear, in view of the natural tendencies of their hearts and of their lack of spiritual discernment and spiritual understanding, that like the unprofitable servant they will hide their "pound" and let it lie idle, that they will apply their wealth in the wrong direction, or that they will squander it, unless they are taught to see their responsibility and are carefully taught the proper use of the wealth which God has placed at their disposal? Surely, we cannot be too careful or too diligent in training our children for their responsible duties in life.

The Requirements of the Covenant

This idea very naturally leads on to our *third* consideration. The necessity of Christian education also follows from the requirements of the covenant. God requires of covenant children that they believe in Jesus Christ unto salvation and that they turn from sin to holiness, i.e., follow the highway of sanctification through life. It is a very comprehensive requirement, the nature of which ought to be well understood. Hence the need of Christian education.

Faith is required in the children of the covenant. Faith, first of all, is a receptive organ by which they lay hold on Christ and all the blessings of salvation. This faith may not be a bare intellectual assent to the claims of Christ or a mere stirring of the emotions resulting from an impassioned plea or, finally, a momentary impulsive choice under high psychological pressure. Rather, arising out of a deep consciousness of sin, it must be a deliberate response to the glorious offer of salvation in Christ; the "amen" of the soul, elicited by the Holy Spirit, to all the blessed promises of the gospel; the hearty and unqualified acceptance of all the covenant obligations. It is not something of a momentary or evanescent character, but an abiding attitude of the soul in which it recognizes its own sinfulness and lost condition and ever anew embraces the righteousness of Jesus Christ. But the faith that is required of covenant children is not merely passive, not only a receptive organ; it is also active as the principle of a new obedience. From this faith must spring love to God, to Jesus Christ, and to the people of God. And all the thoughts and words and actions of covenant children must be motivated by that divinely wrought love. Then only will their lives be well pleasing to God.

But this already points to the second requirement of the covenant. Faith is the only condition for *entrance* into the life of the covenant; but for the *full realization* of that relation of friendship between God and man for which the covenant stands, faith must be complemented by a life of sanctification. The covenant child belongs to a distinctive, chosen people, a people that is separated from the world in consecration to God; separated, not like Israel of old by towering mountains, vast waters, and arid deserts, but by a far more effective line of cleavage wrought by the Spirit of God. And what does the Lord require in that capacity? With Micah we may say, "to do justly and to love kindness, and to walk humbly with thy God" (Mic. 6:8); or with Paul that, "denying ungodliness and worldly lusts," they should "live soberly and righteously and godly in this present world" (Titus 2:12). The life of the covenant child should ever increasingly become a true inflection of the life of Christ that is born within the heart. Nothing short of the perfect life is its grand ideal.

Now surely it needs no argument that children of whom such great, such spiritual, such heavenly things are required must be educated in the fear of the Lord. Christian education is one of the means which God is pleased to use for working faith in the heart of the child, for calling an incipient faith into action, and for guiding the first faltering steps of faith. It teaches the child to flee from sin and to strive after holiness, without which no one will see the Lord. It takes the child by the hand, and leads him step by step on the highway of sanctification to the city of the eternal King. What a blessed task, this task of Christian educators; but also, what a responsible duty! Oh, for hearts aflame with the love of God, for men and women filled with the Spirit of Christ, for teachers that speak with the tongues of angels, to perform the well-nigh staggering task of helping to qualify covenant children for their covenant responsibilities!

We sought to give an answer to the important question how the covenant of grace naturally calls for Christian education. In answer to the query why Christian parents are in duty bound to give their covenant children a specifically Christian education, we are usually referred to their baptismal promise. And rightly so. But this answer is apt to lead a reflective mind on to the further question, Why does the form of baptism insist on it, as it does, that covenant children be given such an education? We have made an attempt to point out that the covenant relation itself naturally and necessarily calls for this. May our feeble efforts contribute something to a better understanding of this important subject. May our eyes be opened ever increasingly to the glorious heritage that is ours and our children's in the covenant of grace. And may the interest in our schools grow apace, for we have in them the most effective agency to train our children for their high dignity as members of the household of God, to teach them a due appreciation and the right use of the covenant blessings, and to qualify them for their covenant responsibilities. Then God will receive all the honor; we and our children will sing unending praises to his glorious name.

5

FAITH: FAITH AND OUR PROGRAM

CORNELIUS VAN TIL

The first step in making progress should be a deepening of our conviction that the program of Christian day-school education which we have set for ourselves must be carried out. Accordingly we speak of faith in connection with our program. We must lengthen our cords, but not unless we also strengthen our stakes. We deal then with our program but also with our faith in our program. Now it may be said that we are dealing with two subjects instead of one. It may be said that we should either discuss our program as such or discuss our faith in our program as such in order to avoid confusion. Yet this is not the case. We purposely wish to discuss both subjects in order to bring out the close relationships that they sustain to one another. In fact our subject really is that of the relation between our program as the objective for which we strive and our faith as the subjective power by which we seek to realize our program. We shall try to bring out something of the close relation between the depth of our faith and height and breadth of our program.

Then, too, since it is the relationship of our faith to our program and not our program as such that we are concerned about, we can conveniently take three outstanding characteristics of faith in order to discuss the significance of each of these in connection with our program. In the first section we will speak of the *obedience* of faith. In this section we shall have to go back into the past in order to see what program God set for man and how he wanted man to realize that program when he was first placed in paradise. In the second section we will speak of the *patience* of faith. In this section we shall have to live in the present in order to see how God wants man to carry through the program originally set for him in spite of the opposition of the evil one. In the third section we will speak of the *hope* of faith. In this section we shall have to look into the future in order to see that man is actually going to realize the program God originally set for him even though it does not seem so now.

I. The Obedience of Faith

When we speak of the program that we have for our Christian schools we use the term program in the most comprehensive sense. We do not refer to activity only. We include in the idea of program the whole ideal that we have set for ourselves with Christian education. And the ideal that we have set for ourselves with Christian education is but a part of the ideal we have set for ourselves with respect to the whole of human life. We speak of the ideal of life as a whole when we speak of our program because it is in part through education that we hope to realize our ideal of life.

Yet it is true that we speak of this ideal now more from the point of view of action than from the point of view of thought. We wish to discuss what it is that we strive for, what it is that we strain our wills for. We may accordingly speak of this ideal as the *ethical* ideal for man.

The Absolute Ethical Ideal

Now if we would seek to characterize this ethical ideal for man in one word we may say that it is *absolute*. We are seeking to build the fully perfect man and the fully perfect creation. We are seeking to build the fully developed man and the fully developed creation.

In theological language we speak of these matters by saying that man was created perfect in paradise and that he was placed as God's prophet, priest, and king in the midst of the world. When we have said this, we have clearly indicated that according to our conception God gave man a work to do and a task to accomplish. Man was to bring out to the full all the powers and capacities that God had placed in him and in the world about him. That man was created perfect has therefore never meant to the mind of the church that he was to be static. The idea of a static perfection is not found in Scripture. If we must use the popular term *dynamic*, it is well; in Scripture only, in its idea of a created personality only, is there any dynamic at all.

But now for the sake of comprehensiveness and for the sake of putting it in psychological language that is ready to hand for pedagogical purposes, we would include all that we have said so far with respect to the task of man under the idea of the development of personality. We must show that as Christians we have a distinct psychology as well as a distinct ethics at the basis of our program of education.

We may say that the whole of man's task was the development of his personality. Since man is representative of the whole creation of God, it is evident that by putting the matter in this way we have not excluded anything that could possibly be thought of as man's task. If man developed his personality, he would at the same time develop the whole of the creation of God. In this way we have also woven the covenant idea into the very warp and woof of our educational program.

Particular mention should be made of the fact that in this way we have not only a distinct ethics and a distinct psychology but also a distinct sociology at the basis of our educational effort. When we speak of the development of his personality as the supreme and only task of man, we speak of man *generically*. One generation would seek to develop the personalities of the next till all those whom God would call should stand side by side as an army with banners.

Such, in general terms, is the absolute ideal which God had set for man in paradise. We may, if we wish, speak of this ideal or program as the kingdom of God. Rather than forfeit the use of the phrase *kingdom of God* because it is in our day so easily interpreted in a Modernist sense, we would seek to give that phrase the truly Christian connotation once more. By the kingdom of God we would signify the objective or ideal for which God wanted man to strive with all the power of his will.

But in order to build our house upon a rock we must go back still another step. Back of our Christian pedagogy lies a Christian sociology, a Christian psychology and a Christian ethics. But back of all these lies a Christian theory of reality, a Christian metaphysics. The sum and substance of our Christian metaphysics is the *creation* idea, the creation of the world by an absolutely self-sufficient God. Now, it is but natural that if God is, and was at the time of creation, the absolute God, then he should set for man the ideal of the realization of an absolute kingdom on earth. By that we mean that God would naturally wish man to realize, as far as this was possible for a creature in a created universe, a self-conscious reflex of his own glory. And this also sheds a further light upon what we mean by man's absolute ethical ideal. It is not absolute in the sense in which God is absolute, but it is absolute in the sense that only the highest possible development of all his powers for the glory of the absolute God could possibly be the ideal that God would set for his rational creature. The absolute ideal or program for man is the logical outcome of the theism that lies at the foundation of Christianity.

Analogical Action

So then we have before us in broad outline the ideal for which man ought to strive. We have seen that our educational objective is the logical conclusion of our most basic convictions with respect to the nature of man and the world. And all this we have regarded from the objective side. That is, we have looked at it as an ideal that lay far ahead of man, an ideal to be realized in the future. We must now add to this that just as we have a distinct ideal before us, so we have *a distinct principle of action within us* by which we are to reach that ideal. Our educational program is not only based upon a Christian theory of reality but also upon a Christian theory of knowledge, a Christian epistemology, and this Christian theory of knowledge gives us insight into our Christian theory of action.

If man is a creature of God, he is an analogue of God. God is the original while man is the derivative. Man's thoughts must therefore be patterned after God's thoughts. Man must, as we often express it, think God's thoughts after him. And what is true with respect to man's thoughts is also true with respect to man's deeds. Just as man must think God's thoughts after him, so man must also do God's deeds after him. Just as man's thought is analogical of God's thought, so man's deeds must be analogical of God's deeds. We have, therefore, as Christians an *analogical theory of action.*

That it is of the utmost importance to see this point clearly will appear as we advance. For the moment we must point out a little more fully what we mean by analogical action and how it is involved in the very bedrock of our position. We have said that as an analogue of God man must do God's deeds after him. Does that mean doing God's deeds over again? That would be impossible for man. Man is not God and could not do God's deeds. Moreover to do God's deeds over again would render them meaningless; it would be doing the same thing twice, which is unthinkable in God. In theological language we therefore say that God is all-glorious and that man cannot add to his glory. Analogical action therefore signifies action on another and, in the nature of the case, a lower plane than that on which the action of God takes place. Analogical action is the only action that befits a creature of God. And it is because we as Christians recognize that we are creatures of God that we also believe in the analogical theory of action. Moreover, it is only Christians that recognize that they are creatures of God, and therefore it is only Christians who believe in analogical action. All non-Christians deny that there are two levels of existence and therefore deny that there are two levels of thought and action. All non-Christians hold to the *univocal theory of action* as they hold to the univocal theory of thought.

But it is not enough to say that as Christians we believe in two levels of being, in two levels of thought and in two levels of action. Theoretically it is possible to think of two levels of thought and action without thinking of them as related to one another. Now the very idea of analogy is relation. Man's action is definitely related to God's action.

Finally, it is not even enough to say that man's action is definitely related to God's action. Theoretically it would be possible to hold that God's and man's actions are definitely related to one another much as the actions of two neighbors that have recently moved into the same community will influence one another. If we thought of man's relationship to God after this manner, we would still be thinking of man's acts as univocal; the deistic as well as the pantheistic varieties of non-Christian thought hold to the univocal theory.

What, then, must we think of the relationship of God's action to ours? The nearest we can come to making this plain to ourselves is to say that just as God's thoughts are the foundation of our thoughts so also God's actions are the foundation of our actions. And it is exactly this that we seek to express in the use of the word *analogical*. Accordingly there are no words in human language that can lead us any deeper into this mystery. The word *analogical*, together with the other words that we use in theological terminology, can do no more than approximate a full expression of our ideas on these things; and our ideas can never comprehensively grasp the truth of the relation of God to man. But this inability to comprehend fully what we ourselves mean by analogical action or by analogical thought, so far from giving us cause for worry, should be to us a sign that we have caught the truly theistic conception of action and thought. Mystery has lost its terror for us as soon as we know that there is no mystery for God.

On the contrary it is our conception of analogical action that gives us confidence that our action has genuine significance. When man first saw the vision of the ideal that God had set before him, he was glad to think God's thoughts after him and do God's deeds after him. Man was glad to act analogically. Man was gladly *obedient* to God. Analogical action is action of obedience to God.

The Development of Obedience

And now that we have discussed the ideal or program in general and have looked at the concept of analogical action or obedience in general, we must try to think of how God would have man reach the ideal by way of obedience. Or, to put it another way, we may ask how man was to develop his personality, the task given him by God to perform.

The answer to this is not far to seek. It would naturally have to be by way of the development of the powers God had given man. And since it was the power of analogical action that God had given man, it was this power that had to be developed. Man's obedience to God had to be still more spontaneous, still more stable and still more active than it already was at the beginning of creation.

In the first place man's obedience should be still more *spontaneous* than it already was. The trial given to man in paradise was calculated to bring out this greater spontaneity. Man's action with respect to the temptation should have been similar to the action of Christ when he met the tempter in the wilderness (Matt. 4:1-11). Think for a minute with what swiftness and decisiveness Christ later said to the tempter who was speaking through Peter, "Get thee behind me, Satan" (Matt. 16:23). He did not hesitate, he did not play with temptation. His whole being was athrob with spontaneous desire to do the will of God and thus to realize the program that God had set for him. Anything that would keep him from realizing that program was immediately cast aside.

Here we touch upon one of modern psychology's favorite themes, namely that of the subconscious. Have we as Christians no definite theory with respect to it? We certainly have. We hold that it too, as well as man's conscious life, was originally created in spontaneous obedience to God. It is not to be thought of as something that acts as a sort of subterranean avenue from the void that surrounds us and as something for which we are scarcely, if at all, responsible. Man was created spontaneously obedient to God in the whole of his being, but he was to become even more spontaneous in his reaction to the will of God for him. And one of the ways in which this was to be accomplished, we may hold, was by getting ever larger areas of man's subconscious life above the threshold of his consciousness. This in turn would react upon the remaining subconscious aspect of man's life by making it, too, more responsive to the will of God.

In this way spontaneous obedience would become a *habit* with man. But by the term habit we do not mean what modern psychology means by that term. We can observe this when we note for instance that in William James's psychology his theory of habit and his theory of the subconscious lie side by side and influence one another. The substance of the modern theory is that by developing good habits we can do something by way of reducing the constant menace of our subconscious life, much as a man may tramp small pieces of concrete into a marshy road in order to make it somewhat more passable. Habit, according to James, is to be used as a tool by which we can make our adjustment to an ultimately impersonal environment somewhat easier. In contrast to this we would use habit as a means by which we can make our adjustment to an absolutely personal background more effective. And the Christian conception of habit works in the direction of an ever increasingly greater self-conscious reaction on the part of man to his environment, while the non-Christian conception of habit works in the direction of the depersonalization of man. True, neither James nor any other modern psychologist openly advocates the depersonalization of man through habit, but we are speaking now of the logic of the situation.

So then it is true with the modern theory of habit, as it is with many other psychological and pedagogical theories, that we can learn much from it if only we place it in a Christian-theistic setting. We should certainly seek to inculcate implicit obedience to lawful authority into our children and thus make it a habit with them to obey, but we should at the same time strive to make them do all that they do out of a burning love for God. Placed in a Christian setting this is not an absurdity but only another instance of analogical action. If man became increasingly self-conscious in his reaction to the will of God for him, he would become more like God, in whom there is no difference between potentiality and actuality. Of course, all this is meant ethically and not metaphysically; we would not think of man ever in any sense outgrowing the difference between the Creator and the creature.

And now in the second place we note that man should increase not only in the spontaneity but also in the *stability* of his obedience to God. Man should become increasingly *self-determinate.* In other words he must develop the backbone of his will. Not as though he was created a volitive and therefore volatile amoeba which had to pass through the invertebrate stage before it could acquire a backbone. Not as though man was created only with a "capacity for God" so that he had to acquire a personality in the future. Man was created a self. Man was created a personality. We purposely use these terms and interchange them. We would not toy with modern psychology's notion of personality by saying that man was created a soul but had to accomplish a personality. We would say that man was created a self or personality and had to become more of a self and more of a personality. Man was from the beginning the creature of an absolute Self and an absolute Personality and could not be created otherwise than as a self or as a personality. Man's God is absolutely self-determinate, and man will be more and more Godlike if he increases in self-determination. To the extent that man becomes more self-determinate, he develops God's determination or plan for him. We have seen with what spontaneity the perfect man Jesus withstood temptation. Now note also with what self-determination, with what sense of responsibility to fulfill his task, he refused to be controlled by anything except the will of God. He slays Satan with the words, "It is written" (Matt. 4:4, 7, 10).

Surely this is the opposite of what modern psychology understands by the idea of self-determination. To do what Christ did, to decide on a course of action on the absolute authority of another, is opposed to the idea of autonomy which underlies modern psychology as well as modern ethics. The idea of self-realization that has played so large a role in modern ethics and psychology is based upon the idea of univocal action. All non-Christian thought surrounds man with an ultimate void. If in that void a god or gods have sprung up, they can only be regarded as rivals of man. To be sure, they may be made allies for convenience' sake, but at bottom they are always rivals in the struggle for existence. Hence man either swallows them up or is swallowed up by them. In every case the development of personality is possible only at the expense of the development of other personality. All the fine-sounding phraseology of the Modernist Sunday school literature does not outgrow this paganism. Over against it we would set the truly Christian idea of self-development by increase of self-determination accomplished by implication into the will of God.

Finally we must note that as man's spontaneity and self-determinateness would increase, the *momentum* of his personality would also increase. As a child walks ever more readily and ever more firmly and therefore is able to carry larger loads as time goes on, so also the personality of man increasing in the spontaneity and stability of its obedience to God would greatly increase in its capacity and power for the realization of God's kingdom on earth. Man would have no "capacity for God" unless created with the knowledge of God; but since man was created in the knowledge of God, he could also increase in his capacity for doing the will of God. Man would strive with ever increasing power to make everything on earth contribute to the great purpose for which it was created. This, as noted above, would involve the whole of mankind. The whole race of man would be as one man in its unity of purpose, in its uniformity of action and in the steady progress toward its ideal of realizing itself and therefore realizing the kingdom of God.

Taking now these three together, the spontaneity of man's will, the stability of man's will, and the increasing momentum of his will, we see that *through obedience man would become free as he was created free*. He would have the desire and the ability to accomplish the will of God for him. He would attain the liberty of being finally and fully established in his willing the will of God.

In a society thus developed there would be no dispute about altruism and egotism. What non-Christian thought has sought in vain, the harmony between the self-seeking and the other-seeking instincts, we have found in the conception of the development of human personality by doing the will of God. Again, in a society thus constituted there would be no dispute whether happiness or virtue should be the end for which man ought to strive. There would be no contrast possible between happiness and virtue; the two would always travel side by side. Once more, in a society so constituted there would be no dispute about the goods of this world; there would naturally be plenty for all, since man by sin would not have brought a curse upon the earth.

II. The Patience of Faith

But how terribly ridiculous all this seems in the eyes of those who differ with us on the question of man's educational ideal. To bring in all these matters that we have brought in, to dream a dream of a golden past, seems to them utterly unpractical and utterly absurd! We must now look at these charges and seek to answer them. We must now see that we have not merely been dreaming a golden dream, but that our theory of an originally perfect man who was to realize the kingdom of God in the way that we have discussed it, is of the utmost practical significance and is the only position that is not really absurd. Let us look at the charge of absurdity launched against our position and see how we must maintain our faith in spite of this charge.

The Charge of Absurdity

In what way are we charged with absurdity? The answer is that according to our opponents all the main ideas we have found to lie at the foundation of our educational program are contradictory.

First of all the idea of an absolute program or ideal for man, as we have pictured it, is said to be contradictory. One will search in vain in the pages of the ethical literature outside of Scripture for the notion of an absolute ethical ideal. There have been utopias enough; there have been mystics who have sought to escape from the present evil world; but no serious-minded non-Christian writer has ever set the ideal of complete perfection before himself and his fellow man. The reason for this is that all non-Christian thought has taken for granted that evil is an inherent ingredient of the world as we know it. Aristotle's mean as an ethical ideal gives eloquent testimony to the fact that the ancient world looked upon evil as an ineradicable element in the heart of man and in the world round about him. If we may believe ancient ethics, man should no more hope to attain perfection than a man with a soiled shirt should expect to purify it while walking on a hot day along a dusty road. The most that he can try to do is to protect himself from the big blotches of clay that fly about as those who wallow in the mire go splashing by. And what is true of ancient ethics is true of modern ethics. James's meliorism corresponds to Aristotle's mean. The hopeless pessimism of ancient times is, if possible, excelled by the dark despair of modern times. The highest that man can ever attain, according to James, is a slight improvement in himself and in his neighbors. Now we can readily see that if evil is to be taken as an ultimate ingredient of the universe, then the notion of an absolute ethical ideal is impossible and contradictory. We grant at once that the logic is correct if the assumption is granted. But can the assumption be granted?

Before we answer that question let us ask further with what other contradictions we are charged. It may be that we can make one reply to them all. If that is possible it will be the best.

The second main contradiction with which we are charged concerns our conception of analogical action. This charge is expressed or implied at various points. It is often openly expressed in criticism of our concept of God as absolute. It is simply said that if God is absolute he must be *All*, with the result that man is nothing and that his deeds mean nothing. Now this charge too is logically correct if the assumption that there can be only one level of existence is correct. But is the assumption correct?

The charge of contradiction appears further in the criticism of our concept of created personality. It is said that if man was a self or a personality to begin with, there was nothing more for man to do and all his deeds were nothing but a farce. And note that the charge here does not merely concern the idea of growth in the degree of personality but that it concerns the idea of the origin of personality itself. The assumption of the criticism is that for a man to be responsible for his action his deeds must be wholly and exclusively his own. Now this is impossible unless personality is an achievement on the part of man himself without the help of God. And again we remark that the logic is sound if the assumption is granted.

Finally we are asked how that which is perfect can become still more perfect. We are charged with holding to the idea of a static moral existence at the beginning of man's life on earth, and it is said that in this way we have made all progress impossible. The assumption of this criticism is that progress must be a change into something that has never existed in any sense. Here, too, the logic is sound if the assumption is granted.

How We Cannot Meet This Charge

Now, when we think of these various charges, our first desire might be to seek to reduce their number if possible. Certainly we do not wish to make our position seem any more absurd than necessary. But it does not take very long before we realize that it would be quite impossible to reduce the number of absurdities that are charged against us. Instead of reducing the number we have to add to it.

That this is the case we can readily see if we only think into the significance of the fact that according to our conception of things the absolute ideal which we have spoken of is not merely something that would have been realized if sin had not come into the world but is something *that is actually being realized in the world today*. For that is the meaning of Christianity in a word, that God's program for man is being realized in spite of sin.

Such a proposition surely seems to bring us further away from experiential fact than even a return to an "imaginary paradise" could do. To say that mankind is perfect now and is actually realizing that still higher perfection that we have spoken of seems to lay upon us the charge of outraging the facts as we look at them. And now I realize that we can offer qualifications that seem to make our position less absurd. We do not mean that every individual in this world is perfect now. We hold that only a relatively small number of mankind are perfect. But this only seems to add arrogance to absurdity.

Then I may introduce the further qualification that even those few, of whom I say that they are perfect, are perfect only in principle and not in degree. But the world can see no meaning in such a distinction. Besides, I do not myself allow a distinction between principle and degree when it comes to the forensic side of salvation. I cannot say that I am justified in principle but not in degree. A man is either justified before God or he is not, and in this sense we hold that he is either wholly perfect or wholly imperfect. We hold then that there are some in this world today who are actually perfect and we hold, moreover, that these form the heart and core of the human race so that the others can be ignored. We hold that when we are training covenant children in the school we are training perfect personalities into still greater perfection. Yes, here, too, you may come with qualifications. You may say that children are at most dormant personalities. This is true in a sense, but it is also true that before God there are no dormant personalities. Before God our children are personalities from and before their birth; we are chosen in him before the foundation of the world (Eph. 1:4). Moreover, I must regard all children of believers as children of God until the contrary appears to be true. So then, we hold that those children are perfect. Could anything more purely imaginary and more obnoxious be found in the eyes of the world than the idea that our children are perfect while others are wholly imperfect?

But all this deals with the absurdity of fact, while in this section our primary concern is with the absurdity of logic. Yet this absurdity of fact brings out the absurdity of logic. For when we seek to qualify further the idea that some are actually perfect in this world today by saying that this perfection is a *substitutionary* perfection, in the eyes of our opponents we are simply trying to cover up an absurdity of fact with an absurdity of logic. Surely the idea of substitute personality will seem ridiculous to those who already object to the idea of created personality. If personality must be an accomplishment in the first place without reference to God as Creator, it certainly cannot be restored for us by Christ as Redeemer.

Thus instead of reducing the number of difficulties by coming down from our speculations about the original estate of man to the affairs of daily practice, we have only added to that number. One thing this surely ought to teach us. It ought to teach us that we can never seek to justify our educational system by seeking to reduce the number of "absurdities" in connection with it. Every important idea that we hold to seems absurd to our enemies. And certainly the idea of substitutionary atonement, which lies at the heart of our covenant concept and thus controls all our education, seems, if possible, the most absurd of all. No degree of compromise will ever get a hearing for our views; we can get a hearing only if we have compromised everything, and then we no longer get a hearing for that for which we wish to get a hearing.

How We Can Meet This Charge

We shall therefore have to follow the opposite method. And that method implies first of all that we reduce all the charges of contradiction to one charge and reduce all the assumptions that underlie these charges to one assumption. Now this can readily be done. It is plain at once that an objection to the idea of substitutionary perfection is only another form of the objection to the idea of created personality. In short, all the objections are directed at the idea of having finite personality dependent upon an absolute, self-conscious Being. If there is such a Being, man is a creature and his personality cannot in the first place be an accomplishment. Hence the assumption that lies at the basis of all the objections or, as we may now say, which lies at the basis of this one great objection, is that *the universe is a universe of chance.*

If the universe is a universe of chance, and only if it is such, must there of necessity be only one level of existence, so that our God concept and our creation concept appear absurd. In a universe of chance and only in a universe of chance will the idea of analogical action seem absurd. In such a universe no one being is brought forth by any other, and so no one can act analogically to any other. In a universe of chance and only in a universe of chance personality must be wholly an accomplishment on the part of every individual. In a universe of chance and only in a universe of chance can evil be thought of as having as great an ultimacy as the good. In a rational universe the evil would be subordinate to the good because the good itself is an aspect of the rational.

Now we ask whether it is reasonable to make this assumption of a universe of chance and on the basis of it to make the charge of contradiction against our position. We would ask whether the assumption of a universe of chance can furnish a foundation for a universal law of contradiction. Our opponents take for granted that they are applying to our concepts nothing but a law of contradiction that is recognized as universally valid by any one who is rational. So we would now ask whether there is any such law of contradiction that is universally valid if the universe is a universe of chance. The answer is simple. If the universe is a universe of chance, there is no law of contradiction at all. In such a universe everyone is master to himself. In such a universe there could be nothing but a Babel of confusion; no one would be able to speak with his neighbor.

Accordingly we hold it to be the best proof of the truth of our position that our opponents are able to make objections to it that seem to have some show of reason. This fact is the best proof that the universe is not a universe of chance. And this fact makes all the arguments of our enemies drop to the ground at one time.

In the second place we would note that when we have thus destroyed the foundation of all the arguments of our opponents against our position we have at the same time destroyed the foundation of all the positive arguments for their own position. We have shown that they cannot interpret human experience and get any meaning out of it. The whole idea of the exclusive accomplishment of personality appears to be an utter impossibility. Personality would have to come into existence by chance operating in a void. Granted that it is rational to think of such an idea, it would surely not be true that personality is a self-accomplishment. And so with the whole idea of univocal action. There would have to be a personality that was wholly a unit before it could act univocally, but it is impossible to get meaning into the idea of a unit coming by chance. Thus the only alternative to our position is that of complete irrationality.

In the third place we would note that with the destruction of the enemy we have established our own position. We have established it because, as we have just seen, there is no other position that is not wholly unreasonable. We have established it still further by the fact that it has now become clear to us that it is the most natural thing that we should not be able to understand comprehensively and exhaustively the possibility of analogical action. Without the existence of a God who is wholly rational our experience would be meaningless. But there can be only one such God. If there were more, they would not be wholly rational; they would depend upon one another. Now since there can be only one, it follows that all other personalities must be analogical of that one God. Hence the action of all other personalities must be analogical action. It is in this way that we would modify the ancient church father's dictum, "We believe because it is absurd." It is the most reasonable position for man to hold that he cannot completely comprehend the relation of himself to God.

Now all this we would include in the idea of the *patience of faith.* We said at the first that we would have to see how the kingdom of God is to be realized by us in the present time in spite of the opposition of the world. Now it is natural that this must be done positively by carrying through the program as we have outlined it, on the ground that it was the task given to man at the time of creation. But it is especially necessary to note that that program must now be carried out under constant opposition. We must build with our trowel in the one hand and the sword in the other. Just as we saw in the first section that God has placed an absolute ideal before man, so we have now seen that that absolute ideal cannot be realized unless the enemies are destroyed. We must feel our strength in the Lord. Then we are able to maintain our faith in spite of opposition. To hold on to the faith, to carry through the absolute program though nearly all men oppose us, *that* is the patience of faith.

And when we have seen that our enemy is destroyed, we can also be patient with him in the sense of long-suffering with his stubbornness and blindness. We learn not to get angry but to pray; we learn not to use harsh words but to beseech in the name of the Lord. We learn to look upon our enemies no longer as those that are to be feared for their strength but to be pitied for their folly. We gladly learn from them in matters of detail while we differ wholly on matters of principle; we walk in the midst of a conquered city choosing from the spoils whatsoever we please, to bring it as a trophy to our King. For that will be our future joy.

III. The Hope of Faith

We have looked at the past. We saw that God gave man a program to realize. We have looked at the present. We have seen that this program is being realized in spite of the entrance of sin into the world. Now we must briefly look at the future in order to see that the program which seems to be so slow of realization now will be fully realized hereafter. We have looked at the obedience and the patience of faith; now we must look at the hope of faith. As Abraham by the obedience of faith left Ur of the Chaldees to go to a land of which he knew nothing by experience and as he lived in that promised land as a stranger in a strange land, owning not a foot of ground, so we have considered *our* program. We have received our marching orders from God. To them we have been obedient. But experience did not bring immediate and great results. The fruits have so far been very small. Yet we carry on. Are we then indifferent to results? Not at all. But we are like Abraham, who not only manifested the obedience of faith and the patience of faith, but also the hope of faith. With him we look for the city that hath foundations (Heb. 11:10).

The Challenge of Immediate Results

But someone will perhaps object to the statement just made that our results so far have been small. Someone may say that our results have been great and that we are perfectly willing to have our schools tested by the common standard expressed in the words, "By their fruits ye shall know them." Now we grant that the fruits have been great. The chief illustration of this is and remains up to this time the little country of The Netherlands. The great social and political stability of that country is to a great extent to be attributed to the people of Reformed persuasion, many of whom have enjoyed Christian instruction. But it will be granted by all that the chief fruit of our labor is internal because it is spiritual. And though we believe that also in this respect there has been a great blessing of God upon our little labors, it remains true that these blessings are hard to measure. They are hard to measure even by those who believe in them, and they will not be regarded as blessings at all by those who oppose us.

So then, we find ourselves once more in a clash with our opponents. They maintain, or rather simply take for granted, that there is a common standard by which the results of an educational program can be judged. That standard they take to be the results in the way of things that pertain to this world alone and of things about which they can judge as well as we. But here we must take exception. We maintain, in the first place, that the fruits of our labors will not appear in their full significance till after this life. And what is more, we maintain that those fruits will suddenly appear in their fulness and beauty at the time of the judgment day. It sometimes happens that the spring is cold and wet and that in addition to all this a hailstorm sets back the crops. Yet to the great surprise of all the autumn will bring an abundance of fruits. Now this is true in a much greater degree in the realm of spiritual things. In this world there is opposition from without and opposition from within while we build our program. Hailstorms descend upon us and cut all things level with the ground. There is very little in the way of fruitage that can be seen. Yet we know that when all the opposition of sin will be removed and the sunshine of the Son of Righteousness will shine upon it all the time, then there will be such fruitage as has never been seen in this world.

And as in the case of our claim for the present actual existence of a perfect humanity we made it abundantly plain that our sole reliance was upon the substitutionary work of Christ, so we must now once more emphasize that the guarantee of the future realization of our program rests upon the selfsame foundation. Paul insists that those whom Christ has justified, that is made perfect forensically, he will also glorify, that is, make perfect ethically and in full degree (Rom. 8:30). And that he thinks of all this organically and comprehensively appears again and again when he speaks of those that are redeemed in terms of the body of Christ and when he speaks of the whole creation being given over by the Son to the Father so that God may be all in all (I Cor. 15:28). In consonance with this we have in the book of Revelation the picture of the new Jerusalem in which there is not a single discord while the glory of the nations, all that mankind has accomplished in its realization of the program given it by God to perform, is brought into it.

Then, in the second place, we maintain that because our opponents look at this life only, they cannot judge concerning the fruit that our activity has produced even as it pertains to this life. What one thinks to be most useful in this life depends upon the configuration in which this life is set. If one regards this life as primarily a preparation for eternity, he will regard it a great fruit even for this life if through the agency of Christian education a good foundation has been laid for the life to come. If, on the other hand, one does not regard this life as a preparation for eternity, any effort to prepare for eternity will be regarded as that much waste of energy at best. The charge that other-worldliness makes us unfit for the tasks of this world is very common even today.

Thus we see that the final test cannot be an immediate and external one. True, Christ says, "By their fruits ye shall know them" (Matt. 7:20). Moreover he tells us to let our light shine before men that others may be led to him. And all this presupposes that men can see something of this light when it shines. But this cannot mean that all men can fully judge the fruits of our lives unless Jesus' own words, that only the regenerate can see the kingdom of God (John 3:3), fall to the ground. Only a small degree of the internal perfection of which we speak ever appears to men, and even this small degree men do not easily see because of the tares that resemble the wheat. And if in spite of all this we are still warned to let our light shine before men, we have simply to obey Christ's command, trusting that God will use even our small ray of light to bring others out of darkness to himself. Therefore we should no more expect to be justified in our educational policy before the final judgment day than the church of Christ should expect to be vindicated in the eyes of the world prior to that last day.

Our Concept of Results

What then do we desire for the future? We desire of course more momentum for our movement. But how shall we attain to this? Our answer to this question must be twofold: in the first place negative and in the second place positive.

Negatively, we may affirm that our hope for the future cannot be found chiefly in the possibility that as time goes on men will be more readily convinced of the reasonableness of our program. In fact we may expect the very contrary to this. As time goes on we hope and expect that the idea of a separate and distinct program for Christian people, and therefore a separate and distinct program for their education, will come home with increasing fulness to all that name the name of Christ. The whole meaning of Christianity is already far more definite to both its adherents and its opponents than it has ever been before. Hence the battle is today more pointed than it has ever been before. Hence also we may expect the heat of the battle to increase in the future. It is now and will be even more so a fight to the death.

Our program, we have seen, is an absolute one; and an absolute program can never be reached by compromise of any sort. An absolute program can only be realized if the enemy is destroyed. We have found that we would be able to maintain the faith in our program in no other way than by the destruction of the enemy. We cannot believe in our program and we do not believe in our program, if we look at it merely as something that is somewhat better than the program of our enemies. What holds for the patience of our faith holds equally for the hope of our faith. Negatively, our hope for the future lies in the conviction that our enemies *will be* destroyed. In the first part of our discussion we saw that only by obedience can we enter upon the fulfillment of the ideal. It is only by obedience that we can have the vision of the absolute ideal. Then in the second part we saw that the choice between our program and the program of our enemies is not that of choice between two possibilities but a choice between a program that makes a farce of human experience and a program that trusts in an absolutely rational and therefore a never wholly comprehensible God. In consonance with this we now point out that the hope of our faith places us once more before an exclusive alternative. We have seen the ideal by the regenerating power of the Spirit of God. We have demonstrated that ideal to be the only rational ideal. Now we would confidently expect that that ideal will be realized because its opposite will in the nature of the case have to be destroyed.

Our Confidence for the Future

And note well that there must of necessity be a direct proportion between the obedience, the patience, and the hope of our faith in this respect. Only those that are truly obedient, that is, only those who are truly spontaneous in their obedience and truly stable in their obedience will really see the "absolute otherness" of our ideal and will therefore see that this wholly other ideal must, if it is the true ideal at all, be the only rational ideal. It is only if we see that our ideal is the only rational ideal that we will be convinced that it will fully conquer in the end. It is that which gives us courage to labor on even though, as far as immediate results are concerned, we seem to make little progress. It gives us something of the courage of an Athanasius who would stand for his convictions though the whole world were against him. Who will deny that it is this sort of courage that we need more and more? We need men and women on our teaching staffs that are intelligently unafraid. We need men and women on our teaching staffs who are confident of their own regeneration, who gladly work for the realization of an ideal that the world ridicules. We need men and women on our teaching staffs who understand the Christian philosophy of education, and also the anti-Christian philosophy of education that controls the pedagogy of our day. Such teachers will have the power of discrimination that is so all-important for their task. They will be able to take of the spoils of Egypt without afterwards yearning for the fleshpots of that false fatherland.

And what is true of the teachers is true also of the ministers with whom the teachers must cooperate. We need ministers who believe in Christian education not only after a fashion but with all the passion of their souls. We need ministers who not only say that Christian education is a *nice* thing, a sort of luxury, but who say and show with their deeds that they believe Christian education to be the only education that is fit for a covenant child. I speak of this with shame. Must we as ministers of the gospel lag behind in our grasp of the rationale of Christian education? Must we who preach the gospel of redemption from eternal woe be told that this gospel of redemption implies the destruction of sin along the whole front of our conscious lives? And who of us will say that there is not a great field yet to be conquered by us in the way of a deeper grasp of the truth and the power of victory in the Christian faith which we have embraced? And think not that I forget the person who is neither teacher nor preacher. All of us must stand together as one man. In this day when boundaries between the believer and the unbeliever are so generally wiped away, we should seek to mark those boundaries anew and mark them well. We should seek to mark these boundaries not with chalk that disappears with the first rainstorm that comes, but we should try to mark these boundaries with indelible ink on the hearts of those who believe.

And thus we have by implication also touched upon the positive aspect of the question how we are to gain momentum for our cause in the future. Perhaps some of you have already become impatient and have asked when we are to come to the constructive side of the matter. You do not like this emphasis upon the necessity of destroying the enemy. You would rather hear something about building the walls of Jerusalem and erecting the temple of God. Well, all we need to say about the constructive side has already been said. We mean by that that our constructive program is nothing else but carrying through, as far as we can, in this world of sin the program that God gave man to do in paradise. That program, we have seen, is the realization of the personality of man and thus the realization of all the powers that God has laid in his creation. We are only beginning to see what that implies. Eye hath not seen and ear hath not heard all the glory that is laid up for us. A glimpse of it we have tried to see. But our vision will increase only if our obedience increases. It is faith that builds our program because without faith we cannot even see it. But now within this vale of tears it is only with great difficulty that we even maintain our faith; how then shall we expect that in this life we shall see much of the turrets of the temple of God? We are building under terrible pressure. There is only now and then a Columbus in our midst who sees the vision of the shore that he has never seen, who checks our mutiny, who makes us work by glimpses of the reward that awaits us. Our chief business in this world will be to pull for the shore. Our chief energy must still be expended in fighting the waves and the billows that would swallow us up. It is not till the haven is reached and the danger fully past that the foundation will be solid and our work will stand. Through many tribulations we must enter into glory, but into glory we will enter and the works of our hands do follow after us. Such is the promise of our God.

6

AUTHORITY: THE CHRISTIAN SCHOOL AND AUTHORITY

LOUIS BERKHOF

The idea of authority does not appeal to the common mind. There has been a very persistent demand in many circles that from the bride's marriage vows the words "and obey" be omitted. The modern woman considers it degrading that she must submit to the will of her husband in all things that are good and lawful. She craves a freedom that is more in harmony with the spirit of the age.

In view of the prevailing restiveness, even in the home circles, it is no wonder that the spirit of independence has also entered the circles of minors. They often rebel against the yoke of parental authority, even when it is exercised with the greatest love and forbearance. They complain that the parents do not understand them and violate their rights. They protest against the infringement of their liberty and the limitation of their pleasures and often break away to follow their own sweet wills.

In the world of labor the same opposition to authority is in evidence. The laboring man resents the authority of the employer to dictate the terms of labor. He himself claims the right to determine the hours of labor, the amount of work that may be done in a day, and the wages that must be paid. The revolt against authority often assumes dangerous proportions in the industrial world.

The same tendency is becoming increasingly apparent in national life. The people have no patience with emperors or kings or even presidents that rule by the grace of God. It is assumed as a matter of course that autocracy must make place for democracy in the absolute sense of the word. The will of the people must be supreme. Those in office are merely the servants of the people and must see to it that the popular will is carried out. Whatever the people in general may think of the first part of the French slogan of revolutionary days, "No God, no master," it admits of no doubt that they readily chime in with the last part.

My subject is not only unpopular, it is also of rather uncertain import. It may involve any one of several questions. It may call for an answer to the question whether the school, and in this case specifically the Christian school, can speak with authority and compel active concurrence with its teachings. But it is also possible that it seeks a reply to the query whether the teachings of the Christian school are or should be based on reason or on authority. Again, the implied question may be in what relation the Christian school stands to the civil authorities: How far should the authority of the state in school matters be recognized?

But the real question is still another: Is the Christian school teacher clothed with authority? And if so, what is the nature of this authority? What are its limits? And how should it be exercised?

I do not fear that I will be accused of taking too much for granted if I simply proceed on the assumption that the school teacher, whether it be of the Christian or of the public school, is undoubtedly clothed with authority. Theoretically this authority is not called in question, however much it may often be ignored in practice. Works on pedagogy and school management invariably assert the right of the teacher to make his will effective in the classroom, and to demand obedience on the part of the pupils. And even if some erratic educator should call this right in question, I am sure that Christian teachers would not do so, for they are fully satisfied that they are clothed with authority when they are conducting their classes. Any attempt to prove this point would be like carrying coals to Newcastle.

I. The Character of Authority

The more important question is, What is the character of the authority that is vested in the school teacher? This is a point on which there is no general agreement and on which we people of Reformed persuasion are apt to differ from those who do not share our religious convictions. In order to give an intelligent answer to this question, we shall have to inquire into the nature of authority.

Speaking generally, we may say that *authority is the right to command and enforce obedience, or to speak the decisive word in debatable questions*. The general in the field asserts it, when he orders his troops about and directs the movements of the army; the judge on the bench, when he imposes sentence on the criminal that is brought before him; and the expert in any line of work, when difficult questions are placed before him in connection with his field of endeavor.

Judicial Authority

The general definition given already contains an intimation of the fact that there is more than one kind of authority. There is authority in the strict sense of the word, generally called *judicial authority*. It may be defined as the right to make laws, to command, and to enforce obedience. It is sometimes called the authority of position, because it does not inhere in the person, but in the position in which he is placed. The strong may be called upon to yield to the weak. The old may be under obligation to follow the wishes of the young. The good may be in duty bound to carry out the will of the evil.

This authority is in some cases original, which means that it is not derived from someone else. In the absolute sense only God has original authority. He is the Creator of the universe, and as such has an inherent right to command his creatures. He has no superior to invest him with authority and to limit his rights. He is a law unto himself and demands obedience to his sovereign will. His authority is absolute. "None can say unto Him, What doest Thou?" (Dan. 4:35). The believing heart will always say: "The Lord reigneth; let the people tremble" (Ps. 99:1).

Among men it is quite different; there are various grades of authority. Take the army, for instance. The captain derives his authority from the major, the major from the lieutenant-colonel, the lieutenant-colonel from the colonel, the colonel from the brigadier-general, the brigadier-general from the major-general, the major-general from the general, the general from the commander-in-chief, the president of the United States, the president from the government, and the government from God. Beyond this point we cannot go, because we have reached the ultimate source of authority.

In the absolute sense, therefore, there is no original authority among men. Yet it is customary, and for practical reasons also desirable, to speak of original authority in a relative sense. That authority may be called original which is not derived from any other man, but directly from God. Thus many would say that the authority of the people of the United States to govern themselves is original authority. But we Calvinists, who do not believe in absolute popular sovereignty, would correct this and claim original authority for the government. We would refer to Romans 13:1-4: "Let every soul be subject unto the higher powers. For there is no power but of God: the powers that be are ordained of God. Whosoever therefore resisteth the power, resisteth the ordinance of God . . . For he (the ruler) is the minister of God to thee for good." Again, the authority of the parents over their children is original. It is not derived from the church, nor from society, nor from the state, but is founded in the original constitution of things as ordered by God. The children are born of the parents and consequently the parents have authority over them and are responsible for their education and training.

From what has been said it is perfectly evident that this judicial authority may also be derived. In distinction from the authority of God, which is absolutely original, all authority of man is derived. There is no power but of God. But while some are clothed with an authority that is derived directly from God, others are invested with an authority that is derived from God through the mediation of men. It is, so to speak, at least doubly derived. Governments delegate a part of their authority to their consuls in various countries.

Moral Authority

A sharp distinction must be made between this judicial authority and what is usually called moral authority. This is the power which one derives from opinion, respect, or long-established reputation. It is the influence that is conferred by character, specialized knowledge, or mental superiority. Says B. A. Hinsdale: "A man who has mastered a given subject becomes an authority in respect thereto, and on occasion renders expert opinions; a physician in relation to disease, a lawyer in relation to law, a merchant or banker in relation to business matters. In such testimony as this two elements blend—one of fact and one of inference or reason; and the value of the expert's opinion, supposing him to be honest, depends upon his acquaintance with the facts of the case and the soundness of his judgment."[1]

With respect to this authority the following points deserve attention. God is the ultimate source of this as well as of all judicial authority. We discover a great diversity of gifts and talents among men. The all-wise Creator distributed them as he saw fit. With respect to the church Paul says: "For to one is given by the Spirit the word of wisdom; to another the word of knowledge by the same Spirit; to another faith by the same Spirit; to another the gifts of healing by the same Spirit; to another the working of miracles; to another prophecy; to another discerning of spirits; to another diverse kinds of tongues; to another the interpretation of tongues; but all these worketh that one and the selfsame Spirit, dividing to every man severally as He will" (I Cor. 12:8-11). The same principle holds for society in general. God is the Author of all those special gifts that make men influential in society and lend weight to their words.

In distinction from judicial authority, moral authority does not inhere in any office to which a person is appointed, but rather in the person himself, in his character and talents, his qualifications and abilities. The more his character stands out in nobility and strength, the more he towers above his fellowmen in intellectual acumen and superior learning, the greater his authority will be.

The power so acquired is no authority in the strict sense of the word though it be graced with that name. It does not carry with it the right to command, which is characteristic of authority proper. If it did, it would also include the right to enforce its dicta, a prerogative which it cannot legitimately claim. When a man of science lays down certain propositions, he may expect others to accept them implicitly, and perhaps they will. But in case they refuse, he cannot employ the strong arm to compel assent. If he wants others to agree with him, he must prove his contentions. The acceptance of his views will be dependent on the cogency of his arguments, or in other words, on moral persuasion. Hence this authority is called *moral* authority. It is not, like authority in the proper sense of the word, immediately binding on the conscience.

At the same time it should not be forgotten that this so-called authority may be of great importance. Think of the tremendous influence exercised by such men as Plato and Aristotle, Augustine and Thomas Aquinas, Luther and Calvin, Wesley and Jonathan Edwards, Kant and Hegel, Kuyper and Bavinck, most of whom have already dominated the thinking of centuries. The significance of this authority is enhanced by the fact that the great masses of the people do not think for themselves but allow others to do their thinking for them. The simple dictum of a great man is sufficient for them; they need no arguments. Hence it follows that this authority may be greatly abused; and history teaches us that it has often wrought havoc in the world. Think of the terrors of the French revolution.

Both kinds of authority may be combined in a single person. One placed in a position of authority may be a man of sterling character, of a superior intellect, of great erudition and learning, and of unquestioned ability. If all other things are equal, this will make him a better ruler. He will rule with knowledge and understanding, with wisdom and equity. The people will have confidence in him and gladly render him due obedience. Was it not something of this kind that the wise preacher of Israel had in mind, when he said: "Blessed art thou, O land, when thy king is the son of nobles, and thy princes eat in due season, for strength and not for drunkenness!" (Eccl. 10:17)? Surely the moral greatness of such rulers as William the Silent and William III, of Washington and Lincoln was an asset to them in the performance of their difficult task.

II. The Authority of the Teacher

After this discussion of the nature of authority we now come to the question as to the character of the authority that is vested in the school teacher. It may have seemed to some that we were unnecessarily long in coming to the point in question. But I trust that on second thought it will appear that the preceding discussion was not only perfectly relevant, but also quite necessary for the intelligent treatment of the subject under consideration: What kind of authority is vested in the teacher?

Rousseau and the Freedom of the Pupil

Let me begin with that which is most generally believed. Jean Jacques Rousseau practically denies the existence of authority in the schoolroom, or at least condemns its exercise. According to him the child is predetermined by his very constitution, like plants and animals, to a progressive development quite independent of artificial aid. Though Immanuel Kant followed him in laying great stress on the freedom of the child, he did not go to the extreme of condemning every show of authority in the schoolroom, every attempt of the teacher to interfere with the liberty and the free movements of the child. Rousseau's absolute antagonism to discipline is not shared by later educational theorists.

It is generally agreed that the teacher is at least clothed with moral authority, and should diligently exercise it in giving direction to the lives and activities of his pupils. He is superior to the children who are entrusted to his care in moral character, in knowledge of the subjects taught, in that practical wisdom that reveals itself in the perfect adaptation of means to ends, and in the tact that is required in the direction of youthful lives. This superiority does not escape the attention of the pupils and goes very far in determining their conduct and in shaping their course of action. With the smaller children what teacher says goes, even if the parents express some doubt. They often wax eloquent in defending the opinion of the teacher, whom they regard as a marvel of learning. And if the older pupils begin to argue and to demand proofs, the teacher that is well prepared for his work as a rule does not find it difficult to satisfy their desire for a rational insight into the subject under consideration. This moral authority will, of course, be commensurate with the moral excellence, the real or supposed learning, and the practical ability of the teacher. If these are not in evidence, it will gradually wane and finally be eclipsed by contrary forces.

Though it is generally admitted that the teacher is clothed with moral authority, which is no authority in the strict sense of the word, it is frequently assumed that he has no judicial authority. Modern pedagogy, while avoiding the extremes of Rousseau, has imbibed all too much of the views of the erratic Frenchman. Rousseau proceeds on the assumption that the child is good by nature and, if allowed the gratification of its natural desires and the spontaneous development of its latent powers, will, as a matter of course, develop into a useful member of society. The source of all evil lies in the corrupt society in which the child grows up. Hence the child must be guarded carefully against the extraneous influences of present-day civilization in order to preserve it in its original purity. The keynote of Rousseau's philosophy is given in the words: "Everything is good as it leaves the hands of the Creator; everything degenerates in the hands of man." Therefore he raises the cry, "Back to nature!" and sternly faces man with a "Hands off!" The less the teacher imposes, or at least seems to impose his will upon the child, the better it will be for the pupil.

Now modern pedagogy does not concur in all the extreme opinions of Rousseau, but it clearly reveals the influence of his fundamental position. There is a widespread conviction that the child is good by nature and will, under favorable circumstances, develop in the right direction. Educators wax eloquent in speaking of the majesty of the child and habitually regard it as the standard of all things in education. In the past, they say, the pupil was largely the victim of circumstances. School buildings lacked architectural beauty. The halls were bare and uninviting. Large numbers of children were crowded into rooms of which the very atmosphere was chilling, and they were compelled to sit on uncomfortable seats for three hours straight. Playgrounds were few and far between, and such as there were had a repulsive appearance, so that the children naturally developed into street-urchins. During school hours the school-master paraded through the aisles with an imperious air, issued his commands right and left, and was always ready to enforce his commands with the ever present hickory stick, without any consideration for individual idiosyncrasies or extenuating circumstances. He took no time for listening to pleas or hearing witnesses. His love for the children may have been genuine, but they did not realize it and did not respond to it in love. He was an offense to their sensitive natures. His regulations encroached upon their rights, and his punishments jarred their sense of justice.

Now modern pedagogy demands that the inherent goodness of children be recognized, and that their majesty be respected. The external environment in which children move from day to day during their school years must be improved, in order that it may not have a degrading but an uplifting influence. Palatial schoolhouses must be built that are well heated and well ventilated. The rooms should be cheerful and inviting, the corridors wide and airy, and the walls decorated with reproductions of masterpieces. The teacher ought to interfere as little as possible with the native tendencies and desires of his pupils. He should always consult their wishes and scrupulously respect their rights. The word of command ought to be prohibited in school; kind requests only are in place. Disciplinary measures should not be necessary; and insofar as they are required, they should be of a negative and preventive character. Above all, corporal punishment must be avoided. It has no legitimate place in the schools of this enlightened age. The teacher need not concern himself primarily about training the children in obedience to external authority, but should bend all his energies in the development of independence of thought and action, and of righteous conduct. Let him reason with the children, and by appealing to the promptings of their higher nature lead them to an ever greater appreciation of what is true and good and beautiful. The time is happily past when it was thought necessary to "break the wills" of recalcitrant boys and girls. Under proper guidance their wills will inevitably move in the right direction. The sum and substance of all this reasoning is that the teacher really has no judicial authority, and even if he does have it, finds no proper field for its exercise in school.

It goes without saying, however, that one who honors the Word of God cannot share these views. We feel also in perusing pedagogical works of the present day that, however much they may seek to derogate the idea that the teacher is invested with judicial authority, they cannot escape the conclusion that he has the power to make all kinds of regulations governing the work and conduct of his pupils and to enforce these regulations, if not by the use of the hickory stick, then by means of other disciplinary measures. Now, the teacher has no such right if he is not endowed with real authority. The modern teacher may pose as exclusively the friendly guide and advisor of the children; yet he feels it necessary to exact obedience by barring the unruly from certain privileges or by segregating them in separate schoolrooms or in truant schools, even if only to protect the general interests of the school or to guard the other children from their baneful influence. Surely, the teacher has the power to command and to enforce obedience.

The Biblical View of the Child and the Teacher's Authority

If we cannot agree with the view that the teacher has no judicial authority, but only an authority based on character, learning, and superior wisdom, neither can we endorse the ideas that the school is not the proper sphere for exercising such authority, that the children are inherently good by nature, and that, if something goes wrong, the teacher may be sure that he himself or his methods of teaching or the organization of his school or the school environment is to blame. This whole method of reasoning proceeds on a faulty conception of the spiritual condition of the child. We find a less encouraging but far healthier view in the Word of God. The poet says: "Behold, I was shapen in iniquity; and in sin did my mother conceive me" (Ps. 51:5). In the book of Proverbs we read: "Foolishness is bound up in the heart of a child; but the rod of correction shall drive it far from him" (22:15). Paul tells us that we are "by nature children of wrath" (Eph. 2:3). And of the Corinthians he writes, ". . . else were your children unclean; but now they are holy" (I Cor. 7:14). Experience also teaches us clearly that children are not as good and pure and innocent as some modern pedagogues like to picture them. It is only when we choose to be kindly oblivious to the manifestations of evil in their lives, that we can sing:

> Innocent child and snow-white flower!
> Well are ye paired in your opening hour:
> Thus should the pure and the lovely meet,
> Stainless with stainless, and sweet with sweet.
> White as those leaves just blown apart
> Are the folds of thy own young heart;
> Guilty passion and cankering care
> Never have left their traces there.

We cannot chime in with that song, and consequently do not believe that the discipline of children ought to be purely negative and aim at warding off the evil that is operative in the world round about them. The Bible teaches the necessity of positive correction and even corporal punishment so clearly that he who runs may read. It is only a sickly sentimentalism that insists on speaking of the "barbarities of the rod." The story of Eli who rested satisfied with a word of kindly reproof and did not punish his wicked sons is held up before us as a warning example (I Sam. 2:23-25; 3:13). Listen to a few of the words of the wise as recorded in the book of Proverbs: "He that spareth his rod hateth his son; but he that loveth him chasteneth him betimes" (13:22, 24). "Chasten thy son while there is hope, and let not thy soul spare for his crying" (19:18).

"Withhold not correction from the child: for if thou beatest him with the rod, he shall not die. Thou shalt beat him with the rod, and shalt deliver his soul from hell" (23:13, 14). "The rod and reproof give wisdom: but a child left to himself bringeth his mother to shame" (29:15). If this was true in the days of Solomon, it is just as true today, for human nature is the same whenever and wherever you may find it.

But the teacher should bear in mind that the judicial authority with which he is invested does not inhere in his person. He may never act as an autocrat. Speaking in terms of government, we may say that he is not an absolute but a constitutional monarch. All judicial authority is derived from God and must be exercised in harmony with the will of God as revealed in his divine Word. It is of the greatest importance not only that the teacher recognize this fact and allow himself to be governed by the disciplinary principles that are found in the Word of God, but also that he convey to his pupils the important truth that he is in duty bound to exercise discipline and does it in obedience to his God. He should not rest satisfied with telling the children that he is ruling in the name of God, with his sanction, and according to his requirements; but he should also cause them to feel it in the way in which he punishes the unruly. This will prevent the children from accusing him in their hearts of arbitrariness and will lend to his discipline a direct appeal to the conscience. At the same time he should not be overinsistent on this point, lest he seem to claim divine sanction also for his foolish and arbitrary actions and thus endanger that which is holy.

The Teacher's Authority: Derivative and Original

But now the question arises, whether the authority of the teacher is derived from God immediately or through the mediation of the parents. Opinions may and do differ on this point. Howland does not seem to reckon with the fact that the teacher's authority is derived in any sense of the word. He claims that the teacher's "powers inhere of right in his office, whatever dicta to the contrary may be burrowed from the dusty decisions of forgotten judges"; and he adds: "We need not that any *parentis locus* [Latin: "place of parents," i.e., role as surrogate authorized by parents to act as their representative, *ed.*] should be assigned us by the hocus-pocus of legal or judicial legerdemain, nor would we extend the limits of our domain beyond their natural bounds."[2] On the other hand Pickard in his work on *School Supervision* recognizes the fact that the teacher stands in *loco parentis*, though with certain restrictions. Says he: "The parent alone has the divine right to control the child. . . . Certain rights of the parent, such as the right of controlling the time and movements of the child for a few hours each day, the right of directing his course of study, are surrendered to the civil authorities, not permanently nor irredeemably, but at the pleasure of the parent. The State then assumes the act for the parent, not with the authority which God has conferred upon the parent, but with the authority which the parent has transferred to the State. . . . It is a right of human origin, inferior to the parent's right, which is of divine origin."[3]

Now we people of Reformed persuasion proceed on the assumption that the parents are the proper educators of the children and are most of all responsible to God for the faithful performance of their duty. The complexities of modern life make it necessary, however, that they call in the help of professional teachers. And in order that these may be able to do their work effectively, the parents delegate to them a part of their authority, the right to control the time, the work, the conduct, and the movements of the children for a certain period each day. Consequently the teachers have the same right to command the children in school that the parents have at home and are also justified in enforcing their commands. But this transfer of authority does not change its character, does not transform a divine into a human authority. It does not make the wishes and desires and demands of the parents the ultimate standard of authority for the teacher. This standard is found for him as well as for the parents only in the Word of God. The parents have a perfect right to criticize the teacher's exercise of authority, but only insofar as it does not correspond with the revealed will of God. The teacher too is responsible to God for all disciplinary action.

Moreover, the teacher's authority is in part derived directly from God. The school is not merely an "elongation" of the family, as it has often been called. It is to a certain extent an independent institution, a separate organization of social life. It is a small community with a life all its own. Now we would hardly ascribe to the parents the right to dictate the rules and regulations for the government of this small republic; the methods of teaching, of conducting recitations, reviews, and examinations; and all the different preventive and corrective measures of discipline. These are naturally controlled to a great extent by the character of the organization and by the nature of the work that is carried on in school. Among other things the teacher certainly has original power to determine what rules and regulations are necessary for school life, and to demand of the children that they comply with them. In these particulars he is directly responsible to God and to God only. He has no right to go contrary to the

Word of God. The moment he does, the parents have a perfect right to protest, not because he does not cater to their wishes, but because he does not recognize the manifesto of the King.

III. Exercising Authority in the Classroom

From what has been said several things follow respecting the exercise of authority in the schoolroom. Some of these were already mentioned or at least intimated, but for the sake of clarity and emphasis it may be well to reiterate them. In calling special attention to some of them I shall limit myself to those requirements that are most fundamental.

The very first requirement is that the teacher cause the children to understand that he is ruling the schoolroom in the name of God. After all, only the authority that has divine sanction is binding in the conscience. He should let them feel that he is not acting arbitrarily, and that, if they are under orders, he is likewise. He ought never to leave the impression that in school might makes right. By stressing his own submission to God the teacher may prevent a repetition of the painful experience of that fond father who asked his little son, "Do you know why I whip you?" and heard in reply, "Yes, sir, because you are the biggest." Of course, the teacher should be very careful and tactful in conveying the idea that he is ruling with divine authority. In teaching certain Bible lessons he can incidentally bring out the thought that all authority is from God; thus the authority of parents over their children and of teachers over their pupils comes from God. The teacher can draw the lesson from both nature and Scripture that God is a God of order and therefore requires this also in the schoolroom. Does not Paul say, "God is not the author of confusion, but of peace, as in all the churches of the saints" (I Cor. 14:33), and again, "Let all things be done decently and in order" (I Cor. 14:40)? He can remind the children of the fact that all evil conduct is sin against God and therefore requires correction and perhaps discipline.

The second requirement is that the teacher, in the exercise of his authority, act in strict conformity with the Word of God. The right of parents and teachers over their children is not absolute but limited by the superior rights of God. These are revealed in the Bible. Hence the Bible is the standard according to which they must govern those entrusted to their care. I cannot delay to point out in particulars what the Word of God requires in the matter of discipline, but merely wish to emphasize the fact that all Christian school teachers should be diligent in deriving from the Word of God the principles that ought to govern them in the exercise of authority and in the scrupulous application of these principles in the government of the school and in all disciplinary action. In vain will they appeal to their responsibility to God, if the children detect that this is merely a convenient theory that is violated in practice from day to day.

The third requirement is that school discipline proceed from the right motive, namely, from a love that does not lose sight of the ends of justice. School discipline differs from the administration of justice in the state. Justice is the moving principle of the government. It is true that the state sometimes resorts to corrective measures for the moral betterment of the offenders, but it aims primarily at the maintenance of righteousness in public life, and at the restoration of that public order that was disturbed by the criminal. To that end it administers punishment. Now the school, as a social organization, is also concerned with the maintenance of justice. But the main purpose of its positive disciplinary measures and of those in the home is the moral correction and improvement of recalcitrant children. They are chastisements rather than punishments. It should be perfectly evident that they are the expressions of the love that fills the hearts of the parents and of the teachers for the children under their care. Hence educators should always avoid punishing pupils in a fit of anger. It is better to defer punishment for a while. Let love reign supreme!

The fourth requirement is that the teacher rule with equity and justice, and maintain order with a firm hand. This follows from the ends he has in view, namely, to teach the children obedience to authority and to instill in them a love for moral purity and civic righteousness. He may be so long-suffering and so indulgent that he makes a mess of the important work entrusted to him and that the fruits of his labor will prove dangerous to social and civic life. There may be something commendable in the modern ideal to train the children for independence, but, carried to an extreme, this may prove to be a source of incalculable danger. Let the teacher be firm in his government and in his discipline. We do not plead for an incessant use of the rod, but we do maintain that it has a legitimate place in the school as well as in the home. When the occasion calls for it, it ought to be used, though with discretion and wisdom. Let us not be wise above that which is written in the Word of God and which was justified by the experience of ages. Today, if ever, it is highly necessary that children learn the lesson of obedience to the authorities by which God is pleased to rule them.

In this connection the question may be raised, what to think of the so-called pupil government. In some cases the responsibility of maintaining good order and the proper respect for authority and law has been thrown upon the students. A council of pupils has been chosen for the exercise of proper discipline. In other cases the principle of self-government has found expression in the "school city," the organization of the school into a miniature city, with mayor, board of aldermen, police courts, board of health, etc. The school city also throws the pupils largely upon their own resources for the maintenance of order and decorum in the schoolroom. We have no time now to enter upon a thorough discussion of the problem; therefore the following remarks must suffice. The parents of our children willingly delegate a part of their authority to carefully selected teachers, but it may well be questioned whether they would be as willing to do this if they surmised that ultimately the exercise of this authority would be entrusted largely to inexperienced children. The government of children is not an easy task. It often taxes the ability of judicious parents and of experienced teachers. How then can they entrust this responsible task, even in part, to children who are still in their teens, and expect that they will have a due sense of their responsibility and will be able to obtain the desired result? Partial self-government may have a legitimate place in colleges—though even there it must be carefully guarded—but is certainly of very dubious value in elementary and secondary schools. Moreover, it is to be feared that the children would be trained for a false independence (for their youthful tutors have as yet no conception of true independence) rather than for that obedience to authority that will prove so invaluable in later life and will be as a crown of glory to every Christian child.

No, let the educators, who stand in *loco parentis* and represent divine authority in the schoolroom, who have a proper conception of the difficulty of their task and of their responsible position, and who are endowed with knowledge and wisdom and tact, keep their hand on the wheel and teach the children to "submit to every ordinance of man for the Lord's sake: whether it be to the king as supreme; or unto governors, as unto them that are sent by him for the punishment of evildoers, and for the praise of them that do well" (I Pet. 2:13f.). Then by the grace of God they may hope to train a generation that will honor the laws of God and be a blessing for society. Then Christian parents will rise up and call them blessed.

7

ETERNAL LIFE: THE FULL-ORBED LIFE

CORNELIUS VAN TIL

We have found in the covenant and in the creation idea a divine ordinance for education. Our educational program as involved in the covenant idea is based upon the concept of creation, and the concept of creation is once more based upon our idea of God. And as for our idea of God, we hold to it not as a moral and mental luxury but as the very foundation of the structure of human experience.

Upon this basis we come to certain definite conclusions with respect to our educational program. We begin more and more to realize that we should declare our independence once for all. We should forget the house of bondage and not yearn for the fleshpots of Egypt at every turn of the way. We have resources of principle such as no other commonwealth of education has. More than that. We not only claim our rightful place among the commonwealths of education, but we have a definitely imperialistic program. No mere Monroe Doctrine will suffice. We are out to destroy—albeit with spiritual weapons only and always—all our competitors. We do not recognize them as equals but regard them as usurpers. Carthage must be destroyed.

But if this is the demand of the creation concept underlying our educational policy, it would be strange if we did not find a similar struggle when our opponents and we face the problem of the future. To anticipate our conclusion we may say that according to our view there is in this world and there will be in the next a full-orbed life. Our opponents hold that they do not know and that we do not know anything about the matter at all.

Now, if this rough simplification of the matter in any measure discloses the true state of affairs, it will appear that an argument must follow. From our side we must give an account of the faith that is in us because its reasonableness is not patent to all who look at the "facts" of life. Moreover we are attacked. We think that we see the truth, while our opponents are quite sure that we do not.

A well-known story may illustrate this point. "There was a country where most of the inhabitants were blind, including the philosophers. But there were a few simple people whose eyes were not sealed, and they spoke of the joy of seeing the sun. 'But,' said the philosophers, 'you must not talk in that excited metaphorical strain. There is a diffuse warmth, as we all know, but your talk about a visible luminous body is an antiquated objectivism. There is no sun.' Yet the simple people asserted all the more that they saw the sun, and a psychological committee was appointed to investigate the matter. They made many experiments and in the course of time they discovered that whenever those whose eyes were not sealed said they saw the sun, they had opened their eyes. The blind psychologists felt over the seeing faces and they made sure that there was a precise correlation between the openings of their eyes and the visions of the sun. 'Dear friends,' they said, 'you are suffering from an illusion; the image of the sun that you speak of somewhat unintelligibly is produced by this trick of opening your eyes. Be honest now and tell us if you ever behold the image of the sun except when you open your eyes.' The simple seers said 'No' and the committee was well pleased with them and hoped that they would recover from their sight. But the simple seers smiled to themselves, and went away saying, 'We see the sun.'"

This story illustrates the point that our opponents cannot make their position of doubt or negation reasonable to themselves unless they seek to show that we as well as they know nothing of the matter at all. If one should argue that airplanes are the illusions of the heated imagination while Lindbergh was flying overhead, he would have to give good reasons for his faith. So our opponents are driven to appoint psychological and philosophical committees to prove that we are self-deluded. And the woeful plight of the world gives them a lenient and a favorable jury.

As on Mt. Carmel, then, we meet these foes. We believe that our enemies serve the gods of the Sidonians. We believe that many of our "friends" have done what Ahab did; they have made a false alliance with our enemies. They say that it makes no difference which gods we serve because all of them are symbolic and not real. Consequently these "friends" are ready when occasion arises to harness the noble steed of religion to the dogcart of political or social exigencies, teaching in the name of the state or in the name of science that which we believe to be subversive of both state and science.

What is it then that modern man would consider to be the supreme good for himself? Will Thomas à Kempis be called upon to set forth the glories of the future life? Now, it is not easy to ascertain what our opponents hold to be the full-orbed life, if they believe in its existence or in the possibility of its existence at all. There is among them a great diversity of opinion on the subject. Yet on one point they all agree. All of them are equally insistent that it is not "the rest that remaineth for the people of God" (Heb. 4:9) that they desire. "Our matured age is restless." It "envies not the dead that rest." To modern men the occupations of the damned in Dante's poem would be pleasing pastimes in comparison with the "ennui," as they call it with which the traditional heaven has been furnished.

Reserving this point for a moment, let us observe that, whether or not it is true, as suggested, that our opponents finally maintain an uncertain or agnostic position, they at least are unanimous in their wholehearted rejection of our position.

Those given to demanding the Shylock's price in things logical will at this point wistfully ask whether such a universal negative can furnish a good foundation for an educational system unless there be a prior affirmative. Suppose that you have lost your door key. At once you search that pocket in which you usually keep it. You have searched every nook and fold of it. If so, you have every reason to say that even if you find it nowhere else you need not search that pocket again. But has modern man made such an exhaustive search of the traditional heaven as suggested by our analogy? Or is he more like a boy who in careless haste has cast one glance in a large storeroom and has decided that the key is not there. Why should not modern man take another look at that which he has rejected in careless haste, inasmuch as he has not found his coveted prize elsewhere? Man cannot live by negation alone.

I. Anti-Christian Definitions of the Full-orbed Life

Rationalism

But let us watch the progress or at least the process of the prodigal. We have seen that modern man has started on his way with a cordial negation. He felt sure that the paternal roof was too narrow and too low, both for the individual and for the race. He must get out. He must go "out West." There were rumors of gold in California. It was the era of expansion. With the fierceness of a Mencken he forsook the benighted, bedridden, hidebound herds of tradition-driven slaves as not worth saving and trampled upon the plague-stricken victims of authority.

Modern men said they knew where they were going. They claimed to have a definite objective in mind. If only the human intellect was given freedom in its exercise, it would carve out for itself a marvelous estate of bliss in the unlimited and ungoverned territories of space and time. The few "Indians" that would be there could easily be subdued. Given full freedom the human intellect could educate the rising generation into complete happiness.

Thus, roughly stated, ran the slogan of the eighteenth century. It was the revolutionary war of intellectual independence that then was fought. And the battle was won. Rationalism gained control in many of the institutions of learning. There was traditionalism still, but the colony of Rationalists was large enough to give their principles a fair trial. And a fair trial these principles of Rationalism had. Did they enable man to live the full-orbed life? We need but follow the course of events to find the answer.

It was soon discovered that the struggle against a common foe had furnished the only cohesive principle binding the rationalist colonies together. When the common foe had disappeared, the principle of cohesion had also disappeared. A jolly time they had of it, these swashbucklers of the intellect, vomiting vitriol on the painting and sculpture of the ages. Cathedrals that were centuries in building trembled before the cohorts of vandalism.

Yet when the time of reconstruction came there seemed to be some difficulty. It was easy to ridicule some of the things in which St. Augustine believed but not so easy to give a better explanation of history than that given in the *City of God*. Some seemed to question apprehensively whether the intellect of man, even when untrampled and free, was equal to the vastnesses and deeps of reality. Friction soon arose. A national constitution had to be adopted and no one had power or authority to do it. In desperation the drivers of the intellect when met in Constitutional Assembly exceeded all their delegated powers and provided for a government strongly centralized. The states could not secede at will of whim. Why then should they join? For the sake of life itself. "To be or not to be?" That was the question. Thus it came about that self-contradiction based upon negation furnished the mortar for the imposing capital of Rationalism. It was a *modus-vivendi*, nothing more; the civil war was in the offing when the revolutionary war was scarcely over.

Romanticism

The rising generation of the nineteenth century once more found the paternal roof too narrow and too low. "Our fathers," they said, "have proclaimed the freedom of the head and they did well, but we must proclaim the freedom of the heart. How can we live the full-orbed life as long as our newly erected central government of the intellect keeps making universal laws apace? The new government is as tyrannical as the old. We cannot breathe in such a stifling atmosphere. We cannot brook the Rehoboam's message of the intellect; to your tents, O Israel!"

In some such wise as this the nineteenth century cried for a new and greater freedom. And again they seemed to know their goal. They had men to lead them on. There was Bergson, that Heraclitus of the modern age, that hater of finalism and intellectualism alike. It was this apostle of the Irrational that led the new crusade. Each nation furnished a contingent of soldiers. In France, Bergson himself sent out the rallying cry like a new Peter the Hermit. Germany met under Nietzsche's lead with the slogan of the "superman" to cast off the galling yoke of the mediocre and to give the individual his rights against a dominant society. Austria sent Freud to open the fountains of the deep and set at liberty the captive forces of the midnight hour; the hegemony of the intellect must be broken in the individual before it can be broken in society. Freud drilled the reserves before they went to the front. America, mindful of its Monroe Doctrine, was loathe to join the fray. Yet it was not long until William James insisted on a separate sector of the front. His drive was directed against the "Block Universe" and his battle cry was "Down with the Absolute." His method was hydraulic, that of undermining by the "stream of consciousness."

Thus the allies of the heart advanced against that Hun, the intellect, wherever he appeared. A jolly time they had of it, these swashbucklers of the troubled deep. The imposing statues of Bismarck, Hegel, and Voltaire alike were crushed for macadamizing the Appian Way. The soldiers were to live on pillage and plunder while fighting and were to be rewarded finally with a harem all their own.

But when once more the time for reconstruction came, the apostles of the heart had great difficulties facing them. The eighteenth-century Rationalism had fought against a certain universal law, but the nineteenth century fought against all universal law. The Constitutional Assembly of Rationalism had to overstep its rights in order to frame a constitution, but the heroes of the heart were not even able to call a convention. No one would delegate any authority at all; all feared the capitalists of the intellect. The specter of petrification stared them in the face whenever any renegade dared to speak of constructive thought. They believed in the future, not in the past. They wanted to live themselves out, not to be cramped in once more. Zola became the literary hero of the day; Walt Whitman's terrific sympathy surged in their bosom.

So no reconstruction was effected. The time of the judges was in the land. Surely that ought to be the time to live the full-orbed life! Freedom was there, was it not? So it seemed. Yet there were misgivings soon. The theory had been that all the hidden forces of the heart were as so many innocent victims of the usurpers of the past. Now that these forces were unleashed, this theory was put to a test. And scarcely were the prison-gates unbarred and the "innocents" escaped abroad but they appeared as a blustering band of imperialists out conquering and to conquer. Pandora's box was opened; only hope remained.

Thus we see the bold assurance with which modern man began on his way slowly yielding to uncertainty and lack of confidence. The fiery optimism of the crusade died down slowly and gave way to sullenness; some even spoke of turning back. Hence more and more discipline had to be applied to the cohorts of the faithful. The chaplains of the army received their instructions every week. More and greater sacrifices were offered to that demon logic to appease him as his canons were more universally and more ruthlessly ignored. Rationalism had placed contradiction upon negation; Cordialism[1] now undermined them both by the "stream of consciousness." Well may the wistful once more ask whether such procedure has any meaning except upon the presupposition of a fundamental affirmation. But we will let the wistful watch and wait.

Pragmatism

Then that Titan Time turned the hands of the century clock once more. A new generation arose that knew not its Moses who had led their fathers out of the Egypt of traditionalism into the desert freedom of Rationalism nor its Joshua who had led them into the promised land of the swampy freedom of the heart. And as their fathers before them had been unable to see the symbolism and the typology of things, so these secularists in a sacred land were baffled and dismayed. Were they not the chosen people of God? Why then did the Canaanite still dwell in the land? It seems that all the resources were exhausted.

Yet that is not the case. The age of paradox has come. Dictators appeared suddenly and everywhere upon the scene. Wilson in politics and Stalin behind politics; Barth in theology and Heidegger behind theology; Dewey in education and Dewey behind education—all of them specters suddenly appearing in the gruesome shape of the laocoon[2] seeking in vain to escape and to help escape from the coils of the strangling serpent of despair. Never before have the eyes of men beheld such a scene. Democracy recalls the tyrants in order to accomplish its tyrannicide. Theology storms the very heaven for transcendence in order to free the world from the "otiose deity" who once did rule the skies. Education begs for the shackles of the slave to set its freedom free.

As for his task, the dictator must rationalize the irrational. He must show meaning in a system of politics and social life or education which by its own presuppositions has no meaning. As to program, the dictator must be consistently inconsistent. He must go in all directions at once in the name of strategy; he must be either wiser than all men or a greater fool than any man.

Yet the dictator is not to be blamed particularly; he is but the fruit of an epoch; the surging sea has brought him forth. In an age that feeds upon the negation of all that is called absolute you may expect the strangest combinations of freedom and tyranny. Life is then no longer like a river following a certain course but like a shoreless ocean without direction. The freedom of the swimmer suddenly becomes the anguish of the drowning man. If all reality is but a temporal mass of fluidity, there may be sharks in it unbeknown to the innocent rowboat pleasure-seeker. Hence the appearance of the huge ocean steamers, the trust, the labor union, the chain stores; hence the syncromesh transmission from the wildest libertinism to the most rigid standardization of the machine; hence, above all, the mob spirit and the power of the demagogue such as has never been seen before.

Then hope turns into fear. Men turn hither and thither in frantic fear lest the ship sink. Thousands flock to this man here or to that man there saying, "Be thou king over us and lead us out of this." Says Paul Elmer More, "Futility is the final word: the literature and art most characteristic of the day are criticized as chaotic, joyless, devoid of beauty, comfortless, fretfully original, or feebly conventional, impotent, futile." Intellectual defeat and spiritual dismay stalk about everywhere.

> It's all Nothing.
> It's all a world where bugs and emperors
> Go singularly back to the same dust.

The novelists offer no program of reform; as vultures they gloat over the carrion of modern life. And as for the philosophers, they too are "sicklied with the conscious depression of futility." Man is seen "as a slave of his temperament, or as a mechanism compelled by complexes and reactions, or a vortex of sensations, with no will to govern himself, no center of stability within the flux, no direction of purpose to rise above the influences that carry him hither and thither." A la Mencken "they have come to realize that the morons whom they sweated to save do not want to be saved and are not worth saving."

The wistful will ask at this point whether the full-orbed life has now been reached. But the wistful must still watch and wait. We have not yet sounded the deepest depths of the negation of modern life. The prodigal is at the swine trough now. He is thinking with an empty stomach and sees the husks the swine did eat. He has denied his manhood and cannot be an animal. Yet he will go to one of his friends. He goes to the home of the dictator now.

Unfortunately the dictator is a man of the same country, ridden with the same psychologism and historism as those that come to him for comfort. Yet he is not without good advice. He tells the prodigal to forget. He tells his clients that the present malaise is but a temporary depression.

And if the prodigal should then become panic-stricken and suggest that the world itself seems to provide no full-orbed stomachs, he is told to feed the swine again for exercise so as to forget his hunger. All the instincts that clamor like the inmates of a menagerie for the satisfaction of their elemental wants are whipped in droves for purposes of sublimation. Psychologists are hired to teach them this noble art; hence our Y.M.C.A. and Y.W.C.A.'s; hence our Boy Scout movement and the general emphasis upon physical exercise and sport. Thus what the head failed to do in the eighteenth century and what the heart failed to do in the nineteenth century the hand is asked to do in the twentieth century. The prophet failed. The priest failed. Now comes the king.

You critics, now stand by and let him have his hour. How well we all know that a king is a contradiction in terms in such an age as ours, but we will call him dictator now. How well we know that subordination and drilling of the most trying kind is with us again, but we call it sublimation or syncopation now. Let there be no slackers then; this is a world war. And well we know that there are no signs of a full-orbed life, but let us have patience to wait a million years.

Thus the easy victories that seemed to be in sight have receded into the far distant future. Thus also the sword has been thrust into every hand; a nation, not merely an army, mobilizes now. Never before have free citizens realized "how irresistibly a modern government could impose its ideas upon the whole nation and, under a barrage of publicity, stifle dissent with declarations, assertions, official versions, and reiteration." New Espionage and Sedition Acts were passed to make any criticism of the war program illegal now. If anyone will not follow the educational dictator, John Dewey, if anyone dare to hold that evolution-theory is not the gospel truth to be poured down the children's throats, let him be anathema.

This renewed and heavier emphasis upon the enforcement of the Sedition Acts seems to tell us something. When William Bateson gave his famous address on "Evolutionary Faiths and Modern Doubts," in which he boldly asserted that the origin of species is a question about which science knows nothing as yet, he guarded himself against any victory that the believers in special creation might draw from such a confession by saying, "When such confessions are made the enemies of science see their chance. If we cannot declare here and now how species arose, they will obligingly offer us the solutions with which obscurantism is satisfied. Let us then proclaim in precise and unmistakable language that our faith in evolution is unshaken." Similarly Henry Fairfield Osborn tells us that his faith in evolution remains immovable though the evidence has convinced him that the earliest man of which there is any trace was just as intelligent as man is today.

And now the wistful will hasten forward again and say that all this begins to look too much like fighting a losing battle. This military display, this excessive rigor of martial law, and these loud protestations of persisting faith in the absence of evidence indicate an internal hollowness. There must be great fear in the ranks. Yet we must wait and see.

Organism

The efforts in search of the full-orbed life that we have so far observed have all been characterized by a sort of individualism or separation. First the head was going to bring salvation without the aid of the heart or hand. Then the heart was going to bring salvation without the aid of the head or the hand. Finally the hand was going to bring salvation without the aid of the head or the heart. But the program now proposed seeks to join all three of them. All the reserves are to be brought out at once. All the forces of land and sky and sea are marshalled under one supreme command for this last great battle of Armageddon.

Emblazoned on the new shield is a harp, as the symbol of organic union. For *organism* is now the word in English and *Resonanz* is now the word in German. This new concept of organism appears everywhere you go. It binds together the individual first of all. The intellectualism of the old psychology and the mechanism of the new is giving way to Configurationism[3] with its emphasis on the centrality of the human person.

Then further, this concept of the organism is to bind the individual to society, and even to the cosmos. And here the subliminal self of William James, though modified, furnishes the connecting link between the individual and the "objective" world. The conceptions of dual and multiple personality make a gentle transition from one personality to another possible. There are underground connecting ways found everywhere. Child psychology has bridged the gulf between the adult and the infant. Animal psychology has bridged the gulf between the animal and the child. How gently and easily the old wrangle about the theory of knowledge seems to be settled here. Are we really gaining knowledge of the objective world? Certainly, comes the answer, for we are part and parcel of the objective world. A new objectivism has replaced the old.

Still further, scientists are everywhere corroborating in their specific fields the concept of the organism. Driesch's vitalism is once more revived in biology. But it is more important that the physicists have realized the dream of medieval alchemy. The very elements are beginning to move and show signs of life. The deadness and inertness of matter is gone. Matter is electricity, and electricity can be given no adequate expression but in mental constructs; so thin has the partition between matter and mind become.

And further still the emissaries of organic union go. With one grand *Entschluss* (decision) Barth has ballooned the message of organic union into heaven. Then God himself no longer dared enforce his erstwhile Monroe Doctrine but joined the league of nations. Then all the former enmity between transcendence and immanence was put away because all *Sein* (being) has become *Zeit* (time). God can be temporalized on occasion; and when the convention is to meet in heaven, man is readily eternalized.

Surely Modernism, the heir to all this patrimony, has a message to bring to us. Do not marvel that its preachers sometimes wax impatient at our recalcitrance. Why still linger over the forensic concepts of Luther and Calvin when art has replaced morality? Why not join Fosdick in preaching the holiness of beauty instead of beauty of holiness? It is all a matter of the tuned string, a matter of cosmic rhythm and resonance. If God himself has joined the union without fear of losing his creed, they why do you stand back? For remember that if you do not join on your own initiative, you will eventually join on the initiative of someone else. The intricacy of modern life ought to teach you that. This gospel of organic union and cosmic resonance must be taught unto the children of the nation. Suppose then that you refuse to have your children taught these doctrines; you would become dangerous to the state and would have to be dealt with accordingly. The state will have to extend its kind paternalistic hand to you to lead you gently and irresistibly into line.

II. The Christian Definition of the Full-orbed Life

Critique of Organism/Evolutionism

Surely he who does not see the full-orbed life here must give a good account of himself. He goes contrary to all the scientific and philosophical opinion of the day. If one still wishes to retain traditional views he must do it with the conviction that the traditional views have faced the same problems that the modern man has faced. He must be convinced moreover that the traditional views have given a better answer to these problems than the modern man has given. We cannot build separate schools for the sake of a hobby. And this is so not only because they cost a deal of money, but still more is this so because we would not then be giving a good account of the faith that is in us. We must therefore seek to give our reason for being out of harmony with the gospel of harmony.

Now we may perhaps sum up these reasons by saying that there is too much disharmony in this gospel of harmony. Or better still we may say that we believe there is no harmony at all in the modern theory of harmony. It is not a question of a little more or less harmony between us and our opponents. The question is where we may expect to find any harmony at all.

To begin with we may emphasize the point already alluded to, namely, that there is too much of the fanfare of war in the whole of our opponents' program of peace. No country will bring to the front all of its reserves unless it is at the end of its strength. Such a military display as we have witnessed of late should bring immediate victory, or we cannot help but think that it spells defeat.

We should say to our opponents: We know very well what measures of discipline you have used upon your troops to bring them into line. Your discipline has become more rigid at every step. Your Kaiser has threatened to turn the guns of his army upon his own people because they spoke of revolution, and men who are leading a full-orbed life do not mutiny. Your chaplains have preached in season and out of season *that war itself is the full-orbed life*. Let us prove this point from your official documents, for it is all important.

One of your leading philosophers, Edgar A. Singer, has sought to demonstrate in a paper of state that the only possible science of religion is one that is based upon the *a priori* of desire. The ancients, he tells us, thought the Danaides[4] unfortunate because they were doomed to carrying water in sieves in Hades for the killing of their husbands. So the old-fashioned Christian too looks for a heaven of perfect rest. "But," says Singer, "it is exactly this prospect of eternal peace that troubles a matured age." "For it is Kant who first perceives the divine to be all too human, if it be not for us humans *eine reine Idee*" (a pure idea, a strictly hypothetical concept, *ed.*). There is the crux of the matter. Modern man does not wish to attain, but only to advance. "Neither for the Danaides of old nor for the humanity of today is there misery in a failure to attain; though there is hell enough for both and for all men to come in any persistent failure to advance."

But where, then, is the harmony of which you have spoken so much? Can there be any certainty of harmony if at any moment some new and totally discordant note may appear? You do not wish the "ennui," as you call it, of our heaven. It is well. You care not for attainment. It is well. Only, will you tell us how you expect to make advancement in your self-chosen hell? Is not your hell based upon the negation of the Absolute? You have stormed the very heavens to bring the eternal into the temporal. Your god is but the next higher step in the process of advancement. You have identified god with the idea of advancement. But how do you know that there has been or will be any advancement in such a shoreless sea as that in which you welter? All things are at loose ends and you cannot even know that there will be any course or direction to anything that you may do. If it be true that in grammar two negatives make an affirmative, this is not the case in logic. You cannot expect a new affirmation from the negation of negation unless there is a dialectic functioning. And there exactly comes the rub. You have provided for no atmosphere in which a dialectic could function. You start with the void and therefore you must also end with the void. And in the void there is no cancellation power. You could at best mark time and you cannot even do that. Parmenides would not allow his opponents to say anything but "being"; we will not even allow you to say that much. An eternal silence and an eternal standstill are the price you must pay for your idea of advancement. You never have had and you never will have anything that looks like your idea of the full-orbed life. What you will have is a travesty on the "rest that remaineth for the people of God." According to your own words there is hell enough and to spare in a failure to advance.

Refine then, if you will, a hundred-fold by all the intellectual tortures of modern mathematical genius the punishment of the Danaides and you will not even then approach the idea of utter self-stultification implied in your idea of progress. We do not hesitate to submit that the very presupposition of any advancement is the affirmation of an absolute self-conscious God. Without such a God there cannot even be a hell, let alone a heaven. And with such a God, given the fact of evil, there must be both.

So then, if we may now turn preacher, we would say that your gospel of harmony is bound to fail because it has not included God. You have included many gods, but you have not included God. Hence your circle is not large enough. Your policy of inclusiveness has after all proved to be one of exclusiveness. God has refused to meet your conditions of entrance into the league of nations. In turn he lays down his conditions for entrance into harmony with him. It is these conditions which we have accepted. We have realized that if we are to be in harmony with an absolute God we must be in harmony with him on his own terms. Accordingly we feel confident that we have and will have the full-orbed life.

In opposition to this you have desperately resolved that you would rather enter the barren desert hoping against hope that there will be a Canaan beyond and oases on the dreary way, than return to the Father's house. Some of your leaders are beginning to confess that they do not know where they are going. We have already referred to Osborn and Bateson. Let us add the testimony of James Jeans who says that science has "no pronouncement to make." Of course we do not wonder that science has no pronouncement to make. The starting point of the modern scientific method is the negation of the absolute. That negation is involved in its so-called open-mind attitude. It follows that science, unless it changes its method, never will have any pronouncement to make. With the present method it would require someone beyond God to make a pronouncement, and even the scientists are not beyond God inasmuch as they are, according to their own view, bound up with God. And if enough of all this has come to your realization that you are willing to admit that you know nothing as yet about the nature of reality, it would seem that our position may once more have a hearing.

Yet of this we would not speak if you were content to let us alone. But that you will not do. You force your agnosticism upon us and upon our children. Jeans, for example, tells us that this universe has come by accident and that we should speculate no more about the matter since accidents will happen. Then further, with respect to human life we are told that "in the course of time, we know not how, when or why, one of these cooling fragments gave birth to life." It is thus that the humble scientist who pretends to be satisfied with searching the facts in the laboratory suddenly turns philosopher, theologian, teacher, and preacher, pouring down our throats large doses of anti-theistic metaphysics in the dread name of science.

Here we reach the high-water mark of present-day anti-theistic thought. Our opponents maintain not only that they do not know anything about the nature of reality, but also that nobody else can possible know anything about it. The present-day scientist is often not the humble seeker after truth but the militant preacher of a faith, and the faith that he preaches is the faith of agnosticism. It is this point to which we have seen all things come. The face of science and philosophy today is, with rare exceptions, set squarely against Christianity and the theism that serves it as a foundation.

Full-orbed Life as Fellowship With God

What else, then, can we do but take the sword as well as the trowel? We are driven to a defense of our faith. The full-orbed life, that which the world has sought in vain, is in our possession. We have an absolute God in whose fellowship we have even now the full-orbed life. We have an absolute God who alone can give meaning to all our strivings for advancement. We have an absolute God who alone can guarantee that that which we have in principle now will be fully realized hereafter.

Is our position modern? If the principle of the organism is a modern one, we have been modern for all these years and centuries that it took "modern thought" to become modern, for we have never separated head and heart and hand. And as to setting man in his environment, we have never sought the full-orbed life by separating man either from the cosmos or from God. Our brief review of modern aspirations has shown that our opponents themselves have felt, have admitted, and have shouted from the housetops that the full-orbed life can only come in a union of man with his total environment. Why, then, should we fear to proclaim that we have the full-orbed life, inasmuch as we have the total environment in our concept of God and of the world?

It is this point too that we will have to keep in mind when shaping our educational policies. Our educational ideals and those of our opponents are poles apart. How impossible, then, for us to inculcate our ideals in any satisfactory way unless we have the educational influence all to ourselves. The modern emphasis upon environment is itself a warning to us not to be satisfied with injecting a grain of religion here and there in cooperation with an educational program that is radically opposed to our own. Then too, the fact that the emphasis is no longer upon the liberation of the head or the heart or the hand alone but upon the liberation of the whole personality, and the boldness with which this liberation is proclaimed, ought to make us realize anew the extent to which the secularism of our age has advanced. The questionnaires that indicate a decrease in references to Deity in the readers used in schools today find their explanation in the movement we have traced above.

How glorious a task it must be, then, to teach in a Christian school! It is in the educational field that the struggle for or against God is being decided today. Teachers fight on the most dangerous sector of the front.

NOTES

Chapter 1

1. Nahum 1:15
2. Zephaniah 1:12
3. D. C. Macintosh, *Religious Realism* (New York: Macmillan, 1931), p. 5.
4. Surd: in mathematics, an irrational number; metaphorically, an element of reality incapable of rational explanation.
5. Karl Jaspers, *Die geistige Situation der Zeit (The Intellectual Situation of Our Time)* (Berlin: W. de Gruyter, 1932), p. 22 (trans. D. E. J.).
6. Ibid., p. 56 (trans. D. E. J.).
7. Ibid., p. 94 (trans. D. E. J.).

Chapter 2

1. W. H. Payne, *Contributions to the Science of Education* (New York: Harper and Bros., 1886), p. 207.
2. S. Z. Batten, *The Christian State* (Philadelphia: Griffith and Rowland, 1909), p. 408.
3. Payne, *Contributions*, pp. 213f.

Chapter 3

1. At this point Van Til noted in the margin of his copy: "The Trinity is not sufficiently stressed in this address."
2. The Westminster Confession of Faith (1647) says, "The authority of the Holy Scripture, for which it ought to be believed, and obeyed, depends not upon the testimony of any man, or church; but wholly upon God (who is truth itself) the author thereof: and therefore it is to be received, because it is the Word of God. . . . our full persuasion and assurance of the infallible truth and divine authority thereof, is from the inward work of the Holy Spirit bearing witness by and with the Word in our hearts."

Chapter 4

1. Charles Hodge, *Systematic Theology*. 3 vols. (1872); A. A. Hodge, *Outlines of Theology* (1879); James H. Thornwell, *The Collected Writings of James Henley Thornwell*. 4 vols. (1871, 1873); Robert L. Dabney, *Lectures in Systematic Theology* (1878).
2. The first announcement in the history of redemption of the good news of salvation in Christ, in which God announced that the Seed of the woman (Eve) would come to fight and defeat Satan's evil purposes: "So the Lord God said to the serpent, . . . 'I will put enmity between you and the woman, and between your offspring and hers; he will crush your head, and you will strike his heel'" (Gen. 3:14-15, NIV).

3. In the decades since Berkhof wrote, Reformed Old Testament scholars have called attention to new archaeological evidence which has modified our understanding of extrabiblical human covenants in the Old Testament period. It is now evident that many ancient near eastern covenants were international treaties in which the parties did *not* come on equal footing. Rather, a "great king" or suzerain imposed the covenant-treaty on a weaker vassal, promising certain benefits (e.g., protection from invasion by other powers) but also imposing demands (e.g., loyalty, payment of tribute, peaceful coexistence with the suzerain's other vassals). Moreover, these covenant-treaties were secured by sanctions threatening punishment in the case of infidelity to the covenant stipulations; and it was believed in pagan contexts that these sanctions, if not carried out by the forces of the suzerain himself, would be administered by the gods who were called to witness the ratification of the treaty. In the biblical covenants between the Lord and his people, of course, the Lord is himself both the suzerain and the divine witness who enforces the requirements of the covenant. See M. G. Kline, *Treaty of the Great King* (Grand Rapids: Eerdmans, 1963); *The Structure of Biblical Authority* (Grand Rapids: Eerdmans, 1972); O. Palmer Robertson, *The Christ of the Covenants* (Phillipsburg: Presbyterian and Reformed, 1980).

4. Berkhof's reference is to the questions addressed to parents in the baptismal form of the Christian Reformed Church in North America. The third question in the form is: "Do you promise and intend to instruct these children, as soon as they are able to understand, in the aforesaid doctrine, and cause them to be instructed therein, to the utmost of your power?" *Psalter Hymnal: Doctrinal Standards and Liturgy of the Christian Reformed Church* (Grand Rapids: Publication Committee of the Christian Reformed Church, 1959), p. 86.

Chapter 6

1. B. A. Hinsdale, *Jesus as a Teacher* (St. Louis: Christian Publishing Co., 1895), p. 114.

2. G. Howland, *Practical Hints for the Teachers of Public Schools* (New York: D. Appleton and Co., 1889), p. 14.

3. J. L. Pickard, *School Supervision* (New York: D. Appleton and Co., 1890), pp. 127f.

Chapter 7

1. Cordialism: ideology which centers on the heart (Latin: cor, cordis), i.e., the emotional life of humanity.

2. In Greek mythology Laocoon was a Trojan priest who with his two sons was entangled in and destroyed by two huge serpents from the sea.

3. Configurationism: Gestalt psychology, in which attention was focused not on the individual stimuli in human perception, experience, and memory, but on the significance of the broader organizational structures and associations (configurations) in which those stimuli occur.

4. In Greek mythology forty-nine of Danaus' fifty daughters slew their husbands at their father's command, and they were punished with the perpetually frustrating task of drawing water with sieves.